3RD GRADE READING COMPREHENSION
Activity Workbook

ISBN: 978-1-953149-64-0
Copyright © 2024 by Polymath Panda

No part of this publication may be reproduced, distributed, or transmitted in any form or by any means, including photocopying, recording, or other electronic or mechanical methods, without the prior written permission of the publisher, except in the case of brief quotations embodied in critical reviews and certain other noncommercial uses permitted by copyright law.

Table of Contents

Why These Skills Matter — 4
Introduction — 5

Unit 1: Discovering the Text
RL.3.1, RI.3.1, RL.3.2, RI.3.2, RL.3.3

Story 1: The Rainbow Bridge — 6 - 7
Story 2: Invention of the Wheel — 8 - 9
Story 3: Moonlight Mystery — 10 - 11
Story 4: Life in a Rainforest — 12 - 13
Story 5: Starstruck — 14 - 15

Unit 2: Characters & Context
RL.3.3, RL.3.4, RI.3.3, RI.3.4

Story 6: Tale of the Two Squirrels — 16 - 17
Story 7: Journey of a Water Drop — 18 - 19
Story 8: Billy's Brave Day — 20 - 21
Story 9: How Plants Grow — 22 - 23
Story 10: The Laughing Llama — 24 - 25

Unit 3: Text Structures & Viewpoints
RL.3.5, RL.3.6, RI.3.5, RI.3.6

Story 11: The Magic Umbrella — 26 - 27
Story 12: The Solar System — 28 - 29
Story 13: Adventures in Dreamland — 30 - 31
Story 14: The World of Bees — 32 - 33
Story 15: The Friendly Ghost — 34 - 35

Unit 4: Illustrations & Text
RL.3.7, RI.3.7, RL.3.9, RI.3.9

Story 16: The Mystery of the Moon's Phases — 36 - 37
Story 17: Ecosystems Around Us — 38 - 39
Story 18: Lily's Lost Teddy — 40 - 41
Story 19: The Great Pyramids — 42 - 43
Story 20: The Enchanted Forest — 44 - 45

Unit 5: Final Comprehension Challenge
RL.3.10, RI.3.10

Story 21: Journey to the Center of the Earth — 46 - 47
Story 22: Amazing Human Body — 48 - 49
Story 23: A Day in the Life of a Farmer — 50 - 51
Story 24: History of Computers — 52 - 53
Story 25: The Tale of the Fisherman and the Sea — 54 - 55

Unit 6: Exploring Texts Redux
RL.3.1, RI.3.1, RL.3.2, RI.3.2

Story 26: The Lost Kitten — 56 - 57
Story 27: The First Flight — 58 - 59
Story 28: Timmy's Big Day — 60 - 61
Story 29: The Cycle of Seasons — 62 - 63
Story 30: The Secret of the Old Clock — 64 - 65

Unit 7: Deeper Into Characters & Context
RL.3.3, RL.3.4, RI.3.3, RI.3.4

Story 31: The Invisible Dragon — 66 - 67
Story 32: Journey through the Human Body — 68 - 69
Story 33: The Mermaid's Adventure — 70 - 71
Story 34: Migration of Birds — 72 - 73
Story 35: The Brave Little Soldier — 74 - 75

Unit 8: Advanced Text Structures & Viewpoints
RL.3.5, RL.3.6, RI.3.5, RI.3.6

Story 36: The Treasure Hunt — 76 - 77
Story 37: Life in the Ocean — 78 - 79
Story 38: The Giant's Secret — 80 - 81
Story 39: Wonders of the Rainforest — 82 - 83
Story 40: The Mystery of the Missing Crown — 84 - 85

Unit 9: Advanced Illustrations & Text
RL.3.7, RI.3.7, RL.3.9, RI.3.9

Story 41: The Magical Door — 86 - 87
Story 42: Our Solar System — 88 - 89
Story 43: The Secret Garden — 90 - 91
Story 44: The World of Dinosaurs — 92 - 93
Story 45: The Three Wishes — 94 - 95

Unit 10: Final Comprehension Mastery
RL.3.10, RI.3.10

Story 46: The City of Gold — 96 - 97
Story 47: The Evolution of Technology — 98 - 99
Story 48: The Curse of the Pirate Ship — 100 - 101
Story 49: Natural Disasters: Volcanoes — 102 - 103
Story 50: The Grand Finale — 104 - 106
Bonus Audio! + Answer Key — 107
Common Core Standards — 108

Why These Skills Matter

This awesome workbook is your secret weapon to becoming a reading superstar! It will help you build confidence and unlock amazing skills that will make you a whiz at understanding stories.

Here's how you'll become a super reader:

- Ask all sorts of questions about the stories you read, just like a detective!
- Get to know the characters inside and out – what makes them tick?
- Figure out why things happen in stories and how they unfold!
- Become an expert at spotting the difference between real facts and make-believe!
- Uncover the secret meanings of words, like finding hidden treasure in a book!
- Step into different characters' shoes and see the story from a whole new angle!
- Learn to tell the difference between what's real and what's pretend in stories!
- Collect new words to add to your reading toolbox!
- Understand why characters do the things they do!
- Use your words to paint a picture of the feeling and setting of the story!
- Find the hidden lesson or message in each story!
- Spot the main point of a story like a super sleuth!
- Read with power and confidence, just like a reading champion!
- Dive deep into stories and remember all the juicy details!
- Learn about amazing stories from long ago and share them with your friends!
- Break down stories into easy-to-understand chunks!
- Put the events in a story in the perfect order, just like a line of dominoes!
- Soak up stories like a sponge and understand everything you read!
- Use the pictures in stories as clues to unlock hidden secrets!
- Find all the cool extras in books, like captions and maps, to learn even more!

With all these skills, you'll be ready to conquer any reading challenge that comes your way!

Introduction

Hey Awesome Readers,

This is no ordinary workbook! Get ready for the coolest Third Grade Reading adventure ever! Hold on tight as you discover wild stories and amazing characters that will make you flip pages faster than a squirrel finding nuts!

Think of this book as a special key that unlocks a treasure chest of stories. We're talking about exciting lands filled with mysterious creatures, all waiting to be found on every single page.

Ever wanted to be a super reader detective? This is your chance! You'll crack secret codes, uncover hidden clues in the stories, and meet some really cool characters along the way. The best part? You get to choose how fast you read! Go solo or grab a friend for double the fun.

Grown-ups, this adventure is for you too! Join the fun and chat with your young reader about the awesome stories they're discovering. Ask questions, share your own favorite stories, and maybe you'll both learn something new! Learning is way more exciting when you do it with someone you love.

This workbook is jammed with awesome puzzles and activities that turn reading into a super exciting game! Every story is a chance to unlock something amazing.

Thanks for picking this fantastic workbook for your reading journey! We're cheering you on as you become a superstar reader. Let's jump right into the world of stories and start this adventure together! Happy reading!

Your friends at **Polymath Panda**

Bonus Audio for All the Stories!

QR Code in the Back of the Book

The Rainbow Bridge

Story 1

RL.3.1, RL.3.2, RL.3.3

One sunny afternoon, Emma, a bright-eyed young girl, and her playful golden retriever, Rufus, were having fun in Maple Town's big park. Out of nowhere, they saw something amazing: a huge, bright rainbow that you could actually stand on! It looked like a giant bridge going up into the sky.

"Wow, Rufus!" Emma said, her eyes wide with surprise. "I wonder where that goes?" Rufus barked happily, his tail wagging so fast it was just a blur.

Without a second thought, Emma grabbed Rufus's leash and they both started walking up the rainbow bridge. As they got higher, the park looked like a tiny green toy set. From the rainbow bridge, they could see their whole town, the rooftops sparkling in the sun.

Halfway up, they met a big friendly cloud with a face. "Hello!" he boomed out. "My name's Mr. Nimbus! You've found the rainbow bridge! It leads to a special kingdom where everything is full of color!"

Feeling excited, Emma thanked Mr. Nimbus and they kept going.
The walk was long but full of fun. They passed through soft, fluffy clouds and felt the warm rainbow colors on their skin. After a while, they finally got to the end of the bridge.

There in front of them was a kingdom full of bright, happy colors. There were cheerful creatures zooming around, their laughter filling the air. It was even more magical than what Mr. Nimbus had told them. With a big smile on her face, Emma looked at Rufus. They were ready for their next big adventure in the colorful kingdom.

Questions

Where did Emma and Rufus first discover the rainbow bridge?

a. In a forest
b. In the park
c. At the beach
d. On a mountain

What kind of pet is Rufus?

a. Golden Retriever
b. Beagle
c. Poodle
d. Labrador

Who did Emma and Rufus meet on the rainbow bridge?

a. A talking tree
b. A dancing fairy
c. A friendly cloud
d. A friendly dragon

Comprehension and Reflection

1. Why did Emma and Rufus decide to climb the rainbow bridge?
   _____
   _____

2. Describe how Emma felt when she saw the colorful kingdom at the end of the rainbow bridge.
   _____
   _____

3. What lesson do you think Emma learned on her adventure?
   _____

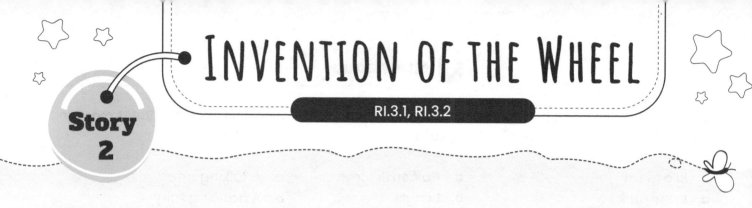

INVENTION OF THE WHEEL

Story 2 — RI.3.1, RI.3.2

In the bustling village of Wheelton, life was always in motion. Kids chased each other in games of tag, elders chatted about old tales, and parents did their daily tasks, often carrying heavy loads. Watching them, Ava often wished things could be a bit easier for everyone.

One sunny afternoon, while playing near the river, she saw smooth, flat stones. For fun, she gave a stone a little push. It rolled so easily on the ground! An idea flashed in her mind. "What if we could make things roll and carry stuff?" she wondered.

She quickly ran to find her best friend, Jay. He was amazing at building things. With wide eyes, she shared her idea, "Jay, imagine if we had big wooden circles to help move things! Just like the rolling stones!"

Jay's eyes sparkled with excitement. "You mean like a wheel, Ava? That's brilliant!" The two spent hours, days even, planning and carving out the perfect wheel from wood.

Finally, it was ready. They placed a board on top of two wheels and showcased it in the village square. Mr. Smith, Ava's father, put a heavy bag on it and, to everyone's amazement, it moved so smoothly! The whole village erupted in joyous cheers.

The days that followed were incredible. Wheelton changed! People moved things with ease, children played new wheel games, and the village felt alive with excitement. And all of it started from a simple, playful idea by the river.

Ava and Jay's invention didn't just change their village. The wheel became one of the most important inventions ever, helping people everywhere!

Comprehension and Reflection

1. What was the main problem Ava wanted to solve?
   ....
   ....

2. How did Ava get the idea for the wheel?
   ....
   ....

3. Why did Ava think Jay would be the right person to help her with her idea?
   ....
   ....

Chronological Order Activity

Write A-E to arrange the events of the story in order.

(___) Ava and Jay showcased the wheel in the village square.

(___) Ava played near the river and saw smooth, flat stones.

(___) The whole village erupted in joyous cheers.

(___) Ava shared her idea with Jay about making big wooden circles.

(___) The two spent hours planning and carving out the perfect wheel from wood.

Moonlight Mystery

Story 3

RL.3.1, RL.3.2

Lily sat on her bedroom floor, drawing the moon. Every night, she loved watching its beautiful glow. Tonight, it seemed extra special. "Why does the moon shine so bright?" she whispered.

Her cat, Luna, purred beside her, eyes fixed on the moon.

Lily chuckled, "Luna, do you have moon secrets?"

Together, they decided to explore. In the backyard, the world felt different under the moonlight. Shadows danced, and a gentle wind whispered secrets.

As they ventured further, Luna's tail twitched towards a patch of flowers. There, right in the middle, was a little star! It sparkled and shimmered.

Lily's eyes widened. "It's like a piece of the moon," she whispered, gently picking it up. "How did you end up here?"

Luna meowed, gazing at the tiny star. They decided to keep it safe. Using an empty jar, Lily placed the star inside, letting it glow.

Hours passed. The backyard became a hub of activity. Fireflies danced around the jar, and the distant sound of an owl echoed. Luna played with leaves while Lily, wrapped in a blanket, lay on the grass, her eyes moving between the jar and the moon above.

When morning came, to Lily's surprise, the star was gone! But in its place was a trail of sparkles, leading all the way up to the sky.

She grinned at Luna. "Looks like our little star went home!"

That evening, as they gazed at the moon, they felt it was smiling just for them. They had been part of a beautiful moonlight mystery, right in their backyard.

Comprehension Questions

Why was Lily fascinated by the moon?

What made that particular night seem special?

Where did Lily find the moon's star?

Time to Draw!

Drawing of Lily and Luna, flashlight in hand, discovering the shining star inside the garden shed with the bright moon in the background.

Life in a Rainforest

Story 4

RI.3.1, RI.3.2, RL.3.3

In the heart of the vast, green rainforest, where trees form a thick roof called a canopy overhead, Maya, an adventurous girl, and her talking parrot, Rico, explored. Their world buzzed with the sounds of birds and the rustling of leaves, all part of the rainforest's daily melody.

One sunny morning, as they ventured deeper into this natural wonder, Maya spotted something concerning. "Rico, look!" she pointed. "The river is much lower than it should be. It's like when you drink all your water and need a refill."

Rico, with his bright feathers, flew closer. "You're right, Maya. The plants by the river look thirsty, just like when you forget to water the garden."

Determined to solve this mystery, they embarked on a quest. They met animals along the way, each sharing how the lower river made life harder. These stories pieced together a puzzle Maya and Rico were eager to solve.

Recalling an old story Rico once mentioned about a hidden waterfall, guarded by the ancient tree in the rainforest—a tree so old and wise, it was like a grandparent to all the plants and animals—Maya had an idea. "Perhaps this waterfall could help give the river the refill it needs!"

With excitement and hope, they searched for the ancient tree. It was the tallest and widest tree in the rainforest, standing proudly like a tower. Showing their respect for nature, as the legend suggested, the ancient tree revealed the hidden waterfall behind its massive trunk.

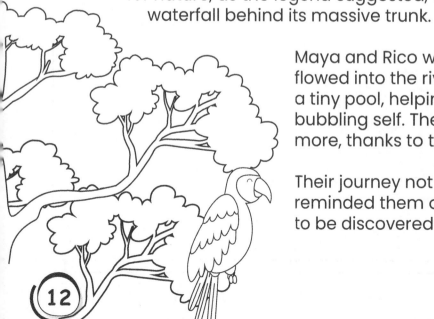

Maya and Rico watched as the waterfall's water flowed into the river, like pouring a giant bucket into a tiny pool, helping the river grow back to its happy, bubbling self. The rainforest bloomed with life once more, thanks to the waterfall's generous refill.

Their journey not only solved the mystery but also reminded them of the magic hidden in nature, waiting to be discovered by those who care to look.

Comprehension and Reflection

What is the main idea of "Life in a Rainforest"?
Can you name two details from the story that support this idea?

Main Idea: _____

Detail #1: _____

Detail #2: _____

Story Mapping!

- Written in each leaf are the elements of a story and its definition.
- Write the number of the leaf (story element) in the box above the droplet (event) it describes.

1. Setting — The location where the story takes place.

2. Solution — This is how our story friends solve their big challenge.

3. Events — These are the things that happen from the beginning to the end of our story.

4. Characters — These are the friends or animals we read about in our story.

5. Problem — This is a challenge that the characters in our story need to solve.

6. Conclusion — This is how everything ends and what we can learn from the story.

Droplets:
- The river is lower than usual, making life hard for the plants and animals.
- Our story is about Maya, an adventurous girl, and Rico, her talking parrot.
- They discover a secret waterfall that can fill the river back up.
- Maya and Rico go exploring, meet animals, and search for a mysterious waterfall.
- All the action happens in a big, green rainforest full of tall trees.
- The story ends with the forest full of life again, showing us how amazing nature is.

13

STARSTRUCK

Story 5 — RL.3.1, RL.3.2

In the small town, where the night sky sparkled clearer than a diamond, lived a boy named Alex. Alex loved nothing more than stargazing with his telescope, a gift from his grandfather who was an astronaut. Each star and constellation had a story, and Alex dreamt of adding his own discovery to the celestial tales.

One crisp autumn evening, while scanning the sky, Alex noticed a star blinking in a pattern he had never seen before. "Could it be?" he whispered to himself, heart pounding with excitement.

He rushed to his room to grab his Star Guide, a thick book filled with constellations, planets, and the mysteries of the universe. Flipping through the pages, Alex found nothing about a blinking star pattern like the one he saw. "This might be a new discovery!" he exclaimed.

Determined to learn more, Alex decided to observe the star every night. He took detailed notes, drawing the blinking patterns and timing each flash of light. After several nights, he noticed the blinking pattern repeated in a sequence. "It's like the star is trying to tell us something," Alex thought.

With his findings, Alex reached out to a local astronomy club. They were amazed by his discovery and helped him send his observations to a bigger observatory.

Weeks later, a letter arrived for Alex. The observatory confirmed that he had discovered a new variable star, now named "Alex's Star." They explained that the blinking was due to the star's unique way of releasing energy.

Alex was over the moon. His discovery contributed a new story to the night sky, inspiring others in Starview to look up and wonder. And every time Alex peered through his telescope, he felt a special connection to the vast universe.

Comprehension Questions

1. What unusual observation did Alex make one evening?

_____

_____

2. How did Alex verify his discovery was unique?

_____

_____

3. Who did Alex share his findings with, and what was the outcome?

_____

_____

Chronological Order Activity

Write A - F to arrange the events of the story in order.

- [ ] Alex sends his observations to a bigger observatory with the help of a local astronomy club.
- [ ] Alex receives a letter from the observatory confirming his discovery of a new variable star.
- [ ] Alex notices a star blinking in a pattern he had never seen before.
- [ ] Alex decides to observe the star every night and takes detailed notes.
- [ ] Alex uses his telescope to stargaze and dreams of discovering something new in the sky.
- [ ] The observatory explains that the blinking pattern is due to the star's unique way of releasing energy.

Tale of Two Squirrels

Story 6 — RL.3.3, RL.3.4

In a lively forest, two squirrels named Simon and Stella lived in an old oak tree. Simon loved to jump and run without thinking. Stella liked to plan and solve problems. They were best friends, always having fun and dreaming together.

One sunny day, they found a map hidden in their tree. It showed a spot called the "Giant's Footprint," said to hide a treasure. The idea of finding treasure excited them both.

Simon wanted to rush off right away, but Stella thought they should look for hints and make a plan. Their adventure was full of surprises. They solved riddles that the wind sang and followed tricky paths. Simon's quick actions helped them when they were stuck, and Stella's smart plans kept them safe.

They finally found the "Giant's Footprint," a big clearing in the forest. But instead of gold or jewels, they found fruit trees, planted long ago by a kind giant who wanted to make sure the animals always had food.

Simon and Stella learned that the best treasure was their friendship and the fun they had together. They went back home, happy and ready for whatever came next.

Definitions

Bold:
Brave and ready to take chances.

Thoughtful:
Always thinking about how to solve problems.

Treasure:
Something very valuable or important.

Character Traits Chart

- List how Simon is brave and how Stella is smart.
- Give examples from their treasure hunt.

Simon's Bravery

_____
_____
_____
_____
_____

Stella's Smartness

_____
_____
_____
_____
_____

Context Clue Hunt

- Circle the word "treasure" in the story.
- What do you think it means based on how it's used?
- Talk about what kind of treasures you would like to find.

What I think "treasure" means:	How it's used in the story:	The kind of treasure I'd like to find:

Journey of a Water Drop

Story 7

RI.3.3, RI.3.4

Once upon a time, in the vast, blue ocean, there lived a tiny water drop named Wally. Wally wasn't just any water drop; he was curious and full of wonder about the world beyond the waves.

One sunny day, Wally's adventure began when the warm sun lifted him from the ocean into the sky. He turned into a tiny puff of vapor, joining a cloud on a journey across the land.

As the cloud floated over mountains, valleys, and cities, Wally saw the world from high above. He marveled at the green forests, the bustling towns, and the rivers that snaked through the landscape like ribbons.

Then, as the cloud cooled, Wally transformed back into a water drop, preparing for his next adventure. With a leap of excitement, he fell as rain over a lush, green forest, nourishing the trees and flowers.

But Wally's journey didn't stop there. He seeped into the ground, traveling through layers of soil and rock until he reached an underground river. The river carried him on a dark, winding path beneath the earth.

Eventually, Wally emerged in a sparkling stream, flowing gently back toward the ocean. Along the way, he quenched the thirst of animals, helped plants grow, and joined other water drops in their journey.

When Wally finally returned to the ocean, he had an incredible story to share. He had become part of the water cycle, the endless journey that water takes around our planet.

Wally realized that even a tiny drop of water plays a vital role in the life of the earth. And with that, he was ready for his next journey to begin.

Definitions

Vapor:
When water turns into gas and goes up into the air, like steam from a hot bath.

Water Cycle:
The journey water takes from the sky to the earth and back again, including rain, rivers, and oceans.

Context Clue Hunt

Read and answer each question using context clues.

1. In the story, Wally turns into a tiny puff of "vapor." Read the sentences around where "vapor" is mentioned. What words or ideas help explain what "vapor" means?

_____

_____

2. The story talks about the "water cycle" Wally becomes a part of. Based on Wally's journey in the story, what do you think the "water cycle" is?

_____

_____

Adventure of a Water Drop

- Write a short adventure story about being a water drop.
- Where do you travel? How do you change form during your journey (like turning into vapor or rain)?
- Use your imagination!

Beginning (Where your adventure starts)

_____

Middle (Changes you go through and what you see)

_____

End (Where you end up and what you've learned)

_____

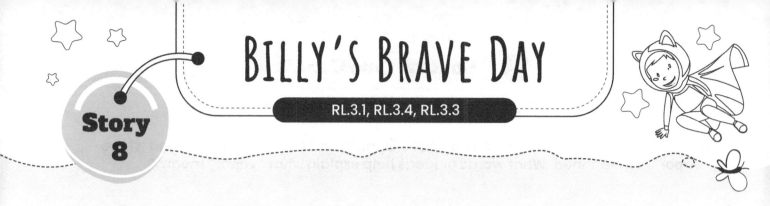

Billy's Brave Day

RL.3.1, RL.3.4, RL.3.3

In the lively town of Sunflower Valley, Billy, a boy with a heart as big as his imagination, found adventures in everyday moments. Though sometimes shy, Billy's curiosity often led him to unexpected discoveries.

One breezy afternoon, while skipping his way home through the park, Billy heard a curious sound — a mix between a squeak and a whimper. It was coming from beneath a bush, dense with leaves and shadow.

Peering through the branches, Billy spotted a pair of bright eyes staring back at him. A tiny puppy, with fur as golden as the sun, was tangled in a mess of vines. "Oh no," Billy whispered, his heart both racing with worry and pounding with the thrill of a new adventure.

Remembering his favorite superhero's motto, "Courage is doing what's right, even when you're afraid," Billy knew what he had to do. "Hang on, little buddy," he said, his voice steady, "I'm coming to get you."

With gentle hands and a lot of patience, Billy untangled the puppy, who, in gratitude, covered Billy's face with thankful puppy kisses. Laughing, Billy said, "I think I'll call you 'Brave' because it took a lot of courage for both of us today."

Deciding to take Brave home, Billy felt like a real-life superhero. His parents were surprised but quickly helped Billy make "Found Puppy" posters to hang around town.

A few days later, Brave's family was found. They had been looking for their lost puppy everywhere. They were overjoyed to see him safe and couldn't thank Billy enough. "You're our hero," they told Billy, who felt his heart swell with pride.

As Billy waved goodbye to Brave and his family, he realized that bravery comes in many forms, and sometimes, the smallest acts can make the biggest difference.

❓ What is Literal Language?

Literal language is when you say exactly what you mean. It's like telling someone, "I have a blue pencil." If you really do have a blue pencil in your hand, you're speaking literally. It's just the facts!

❓ What is Nonliteral Language?

Nonliteral language is a bit more fun and creative. It's when you use words to describe something in a way that isn't exactly true, but it helps paint a picture in someone's mind or shows how you feel. It's like saying, "It's raining cats and dogs!" You don't mean real cats and dogs are falling from the sky; you're just saying it's raining very hard.

"Heart as big as his imagination" — Is this literal or nonliteral? What does it mean?

_____

"Covered Billy's face with thankful puppy kisses" — Is this literal or nonliteral? Explain.

_____

📝 "Billy's New Mission"

Now, it's your turn to create a story. Imagine Billy finds a mysterious key in the park. Write about his next adventure. Where does the key lead him? What challenges does he face, and how does he overcome them?

_____

_____

_____

_____

How Plants Grow

RI.3.3, RI.3.4

In the peaceful town of Willow Creek, there was a community garden where everyone's plants thrived, except for Mia's. Mia, a bright and eager third grader, couldn't figure out why her garden plot remained bare. She watered her seeds daily, gave them plenty of sunlight, and even sang to them, hoping for a sprout.

One sunny morning, Mia noticed her friend Jake's flowers were blooming beautifully. "How do you do it, Jake?" Mia asked, filled with curiosity.

Jake smiled, "It's all about the soil. Let me show you." He explained that plants need rich, nutritious soil to grow, something Mia hadn't considered. Together, they examined Mia's plot and discovered it was filled with clay, not ideal for planting.

Determined to solve her garden mystery, Mia set out to improve her soil. With help from Jake and some research at the local library, Mia learned about composting. She started collecting fruit peels, vegetable scraps, and eggshells, mixing them into her garden plot.

Weeks passed, and Mia's dedication transformed her barren plot. Tiny green sprouts emerged, growing stronger each day. Her garden became a lush corner of the community space, filled with vibrant colors and fragrances.

Mia's discovery of composting not only solved her mystery but also sparked a new project for Willow Creek. She shared her knowledge with the community, inspiring everyone to start composting, making the entire garden more bountiful.

Through her journey, Mia learned that sometimes, the key to growth is understanding what lies beneath the surface. Her curiosity and effort turned her garden mystery into a thriving success, teaching her and her neighbors the importance of soil health for the environment.

Vocabulary Match-Up

Match the word to its correct definition by writing the letter next to the correct number.

(A) **Barren** ☐ The process of turning organic waste into rich soil.

(B) **Composting** ☐ Providing what is necessary for good health and growth.

(C) **Curiosity** ☐ Tiny plants that emerge from the seeds.

(D) **Lush** ☐ Land that is too poor to produce much or any vegetation.

(E) **Nutritious** ☐ Growing densely and healthily; very green and vibrant.

(F) **Sprouts** ☐ A strong desire to know or learn something.

My Garden Plan

- Design your own garden plot. Draw where you would plant different vegetables or flowers and mark where you would add compost.
- Write a few sentences about how you would take care of your garden.

23

The Laughing Llama

RL.3.3, RL.3.4

In the vibrant village of Sunnyvale, nestled among rolling hills and bustling farms, lived a unique llama named Larry. Larry was no ordinary llama; he had a laugh that could light up the entire village. His best friend, Maya, a thoughtful and kind-hearted girl, shared many adventures with him.

One day, the village faced a mystery: the laughter that usually filled the air had vanished. The villagers felt a gloom they couldn't shake off. Larry noticed Maya looking particularly down. "Why so glum, Maya?" he asked with a gentle nudge.

"It's the village, Larry. Everyone's lost their cheer, and I don't know how to bring it back," Maya sighed.

Determined to solve the problem, Larry thought of the one thing he knew best: laughter. "Maybe, what the village needs is a good laugh," Larry suggested. Together, they hatched a plan to host a comedy show in the village square.

Maya was hesitant. "But Larry, do you think laughter alone can solve it?" she wondered. Larry's eyes sparkled with confidence. "Let's give it a try. Laughter can be quite powerful," he reassured her.

The day of the show, Larry and Maya were nervous. However, as Larry started sharing funny stories and jokes, the first chuckles, then roaring laughter, filled the square. Maya's storytelling brought smiles, and soon, the whole village was laughing together, their spirits lifted.

The laughter didn't just bring back the cheer; it reminded everyone of the joy found in simple moments and the power of coming together as a community.

"Thank you, Larry. You reminded us all how a little laughter can go a long way," the villagers thanked Larry and Maya, their hearts light once more.

Larry winked at Maya, "See, laughter is the best medicine."

And from that day, Larry wasn't just a llama; he was Larry, the Laughing Llama, the heart of Sunnyvale.

Character Traits Chart

Below are traits for Larry and Maya. In the chart provided, note how you think each trait helped solve the village's problem.

Larry's Traits:

Humorous
_____

Optimistic
_____

Maya's Traits:

Thoughtful
_____

Caring
_____

What Does That Really Mean?

- Read these phrases from the story.
- Decide if they are literal or nonliteral. Then, explain what each phrase means in your own words.

"Laugh that could light up the entire village" (Literal) (Nonliteral)

_____

"Laughter is the best medicine" (Literal) (Nonliteral)

_____

"Heart as big as his imagination" (Literal) (Nonliteral)

_____

The Magic Umbrella

Story 11

RL.3.5, RL.3.6

In the quaint town of Raindrop Hollow, where it rained more than the sun shone, lived Ellie, a spirited girl with an extraordinary umbrella. This wasn't just any umbrella; it was a magic umbrella that could transport Ellie to any place she imagined when it rained.

One stormy afternoon, Ellie opened her magic umbrella, wishing to escape to a sunny beach. However, she found herself in a dense, enchanted forest instead. Surprised but intrigued, Ellie ventured deeper, guided by the umbrella's soft hum.

In the forest, Ellie encountered a talking fox named Finn, who seemed upset. "The forest has been dark and gloomy ever since the sun gem was taken by the mischievous wind spirits," Finn explained, his tail drooping.

Realizing the forest's plight, Ellie decided to help. Using her umbrella, she and Finn embarked on a quest to find the sun gem. They braved challenges, from riddles whispered by ancient trees to navigating mazes formed by the wind.

Through each challenge, Ellie learned more about adventure and friendship. She also understood how the forest was connected and the importance of light, both real and symbolic.

Finally, at the heart of the forest, Ellie and Finn found the sun gem, guarded by the wind spirits. With courage and cleverness, Ellie convinced the spirits to return the gem, promising to visit and share stories of the outside world.

The forest was bathed in sunlight once more, vibrant and thriving. Ellie returned home, her bond with Finn and the magic forest forever etched in her heart, her magic umbrella ready for the next adventure.

Scene Sequencer

Number the events 1 to 6 of Ellie's adventure in the order they happened.

- [ ] Ellie and Finn found the sun gem, guarded by the wind spirits.
- [ ] The forest was bathed in sunlight once more, vibrant and thriving.
- [ ] Ellie encountered a talking fox named Finn, who explained the forest's gloom.
- [ ] Ellie decided to help Finn and embarked on a quest to find the sun gem.
- [ ] Ellie opened her magic umbrella, wishing to escape to a sunny beach but ended up in a dense, enchanted forest.
- [ ] Ellie returned home, her bond with Finn and the magic forest forever etched in her heart.

Illustrate the Adventure

◇ Rewrite the scene where Ellie and Finn meet from Finn's perspective.
◇ How does he see Ellie and the situation differently?

_____
_____
_____
_____
_____

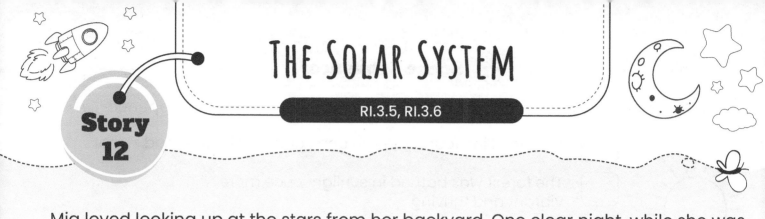

The Solar System

RI.3.5, RI.3.6

Mia loved looking up at the stars from her backyard. One clear night, while she was wishing she could visit the stars, a friendly comet named Comet zoomed down to her. Comet had a big smile and said, "Want to see the planets up close?"

First, they zipped to Mercury, really close to the Sun. "It's super hot here!" Mia said. Then, they whooshed to Venus, where thick clouds covered everything. "Wow, it's like a mystery planet," Mia giggled.

Next was Mars, with its red dirt and tall mountains. "It looks a bit like the desert," Mia observed. They made a quick stop at Jupiter, noticing its big red spot. "It's like a giant storm!" she exclaimed.

Saturn's rings made Mia's eyes wide with wonder. "They're so pretty!" Then, at Uranus and Neptune, Mia learned about ice giants. "Brr, it's cold," she shivered, even though they were just looking from afar.

After their tour, Comet said, "Time to head back to Earth, the most special planet of all." Mia nodded, thinking about all the water, trees, and animals waiting for them.

Back in her backyard, Mia waved goodbye to Comet, who zoomed off into the night. "Thanks for the adventure!" she called out. Mia couldn't wait to tell her friends about the solar system and how Earth was her favorite planet.

Sequence of Planets

Help Mia remember her journey! List the planets Mia visited in the order she saw them. Don't forget Earth at the end!

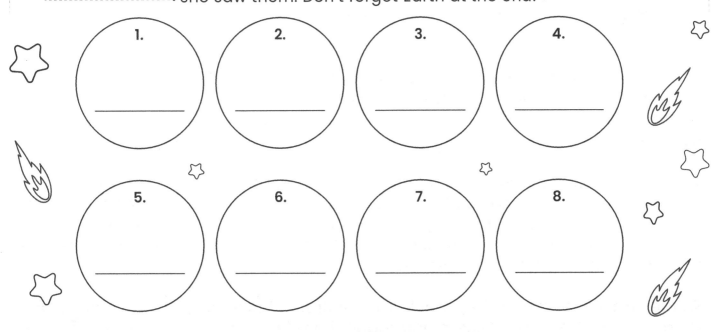

Dazzling Diagrams

Create an illustration of Mia's favorite planet and add a caption from Mia's perspective, explaining why it's her favorite.

Adventures in Dreamland

Story 13 — RL.3.5, RL.3.6

One night, while the stars twinkled above, Ellie and Jax discovered a big problem in Dreamland. The Dream Crystal, which makes all dreams happen, was getting dimmer. This meant that dreams were becoming mixed up and confusing for everyone!

To fix it, Ellie and Jax needed to understand how dreams worked and what everyone was dreaming about. Ellie was brave and always ready for an adventure. She loved meeting new characters and learning their stories. Jax, on the other hand, was observant and analytical. He preferred to carefully study each dream to understand how it was put together.

As they traveled around, they met lots of different characters, each having strange dreams. Ellie chatted with them and made them feel comfortable, while Jax paid close attention to the details of each dream. By combining their skills, they started to understand how dreams were structured and what everyone was dreaming about.

Finally, they reached the Crystal Cave. They put together all the pieces of the dreams they had seen. With their new understanding, they made the Dream Crystal bright again, making dreams in Dreamland clear and balanced once more. Their adventure taught them that it's important to see things from different points of view and that every part of a story is essential to make it great.

Crystal Segment

Write a brief description of what happens in each part of the story.

Beginning _____
_____
_____

Middle _____
_____
_____

End _____
_____
_____

Compare and Contrast Characters

- Compare and contrast Ellie and Jax. In the overlapping section, write down traits or actions they share.
- In the separate sections, write down what makes each character unique.

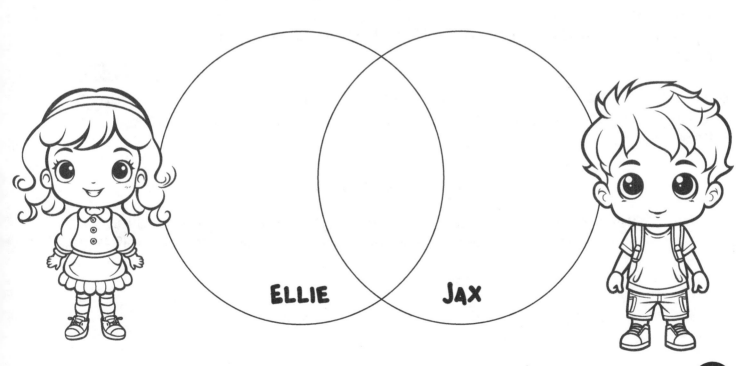

The World of Bees

Story 14

RI.3.5, RI.3.6

In the lush meadow just beyond the bustling town, there existed a world rarely seen but vitally important - the world of bees. In this world, Bella, a young bee with boundless curiosity, embarked on her first pollen-gathering mission.

Bella's journey was no small feat. She learned to communicate with the "waggle dance," a unique way bees share where to find the best flowers. But Bella noticed something troubling. Some flowers were disappearing, and it was becoming harder to find food.

Determined to find out why, Bella sought the wisdom of the hive's elder, Buzz. Buzz explained that the meadow was changing. More houses were being built, and fewer flowers were being planted. It was a problem not just for the bees but for everyone.

Bella had an idea. With Buzz's help, she would show the town's people how important bees and flowers were to the world. They organized a "Bee Day" at the local school, where Bella and Buzz taught children about bees, pollination, and planting flowers.

Their plan worked! The children were fascinated. They started planting more flowers everywhere - in their yards, at schools, and even in window boxes. The meadow began to bloom like never before, providing plenty of food for the bees and beauty for the town.

Bella's courage and curiosity had bridged two worlds, showing everyone that even the smallest bee can make a big difference.

Through Buzz's Eyes

Rewrite the scene of planning "Bee Day" from Buzz's perspective. How does he feel about Bella's plan and their visit to the school?

🐝 Bee Dance Decoder

- ◇ Help Bella teach the waggle dance!
- ◇ Number the events 1 to 5 of Bella's adventure in the order they happened.

☐ Bella seeks the wisdom of the hive's elder, Buzz, who explains the environmental changes affecting the meadow due to urban development.

☐ Bella learns to communicate with the "waggle dance" to share where to find the best flowers.

☐ Bella embarks on her first pollen-gathering mission in the lush meadow beyond the town.

☐ Bella and Buzz organize a "Bee Day" at the local school to educate children about the importance of bees, pollination, and planting flowers, sparking a community-wide effort to restore the meadow and support bee populations.

☐ Bella notices the disappearance of flowers and the increasing difficulty in finding food, prompting her curiosity about the changing meadow.

🎨 Meadow Makeover

- ◇ Create a before and after illustration of the meadow showing the change from few flowers to a bloom of color.
- ◇ Add captions describing the transformation from both Bella's and a child's viewpoint.

Before

After

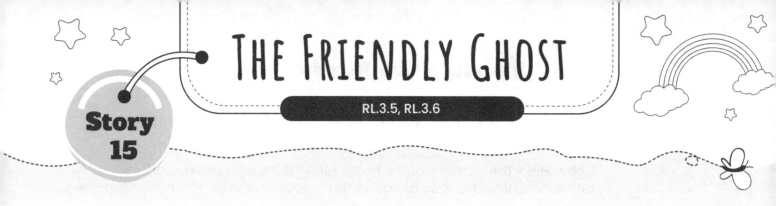

The Friendly Ghost

Story 15 — RL.3.5, RL.3.6

In the heart of the old town, nestled among ancient oaks, stood a grand, yet inviting house that everyone called "Whispering Oaks." Despite its beauty, a rumor had kept visitors at bay: a friendly ghost named Jasper lived there.

Jasper, unlike the spooky ghosts in tales, loved company. He spent his days reading stories and playing hide-and-seek with the wind. However, he often wished for a friend to share in his adventures.

One sunny afternoon, Emma, a curious and brave girl, wandered into Whispering Oaks, drawn by its mystery. To her surprise, she found Jasper, and instead of running away, she greeted him with a smile.

"Why do you stay hidden?" Emma asked.

"People are scared of what they don't understand," Jasper replied, "But I love this home."

Determined to change the town's view of Jasper, Emma organized a "Meet Jasper Day." She invited everyone to Whispering Oaks, promising a day of fun and games.

The day arrived, and to the town's amazement, Jasper was nothing like the ghost stories. He was kind, funny, and an excellent hide-and-seek player. The townsfolk learned that Jasper was just like them, enjoying stories, laughter, and friendship.

From that day on, Whispering Oaks became the town's favorite gathering place, and Jasper, the most beloved resident. Emma had shown everyone that understanding and kindness could turn fear into friendship.

Jasper's Viewpoint

- Rewrite the "Meet Jasper Day" from Jasper's perspective.
- How does he feel about meeting the townsfolk?

Ghostly Gatherings

- Draw a scene from "Meet Jasper Day."
- Add a caption that includes what Jasper might be thinking or feeling during the event.

The Mystery of the Moon's Phases

RI.3.7, RI.3.2, RI.3.3

Mia and Leo loved visiting the park after school. One evening, they noticed the moon rising. "Look, Leo! The moon looks different from last night," Mia said. "Yeah, yesterday it was a big circle, but tonight it's a half-moon. Why does the moon change shape?" asked Leo. "I don't know, but let's find out!"

The next day, they asked their science teacher, Mr. Thompson. "Mr. Thompson, why does the moon change shape?" Mia asked. "The moon's shape changes because of its phases. These phases are part of a cycle that takes about 29.5 days," Mr. Thompson explained.

"Phases?" Leo echoed. "Yes," said Mr. Thompson, showing a chart. "It starts with the New Moon, which we can't see because it's between Earth and the sun. Then, there's the Waxing Crescent, where a small part of the moon is visible. Next is the First Quarter, where half of the moon is lit up."

"So it keeps changing?" Mia asked. "Exactly," Mr. Thompson continued. "After the First Quarter, it's the Waxing Gibbous, then the Full Moon, where the whole moon is bright. Then comes the Waning Gibbous, the Last Quarter, and finally the Waning Crescent before starting over again."

"So the moon doesn't actually change shape, it's just how we see it from Earth?" Leo asked. "That's right. The sunlight reflects off the moon differently as it orbits Earth," Mr. Thompson confirmed.

That night, Mia and Leo looked up at the sky with new understanding. "It's the Waxing Gibbous tonight," said Mia. "Yeah, and in a few days, it'll be a Full Moon," added Leo.

From then on, they loved watching the moon's phases and sharing their knowledge with others. The moon's magic wasn't a mystery anymore; it was a fascinating cycle they couldn't wait to see again and again.

The Mystery of the Moon's Phases

Draw and label the moon phases in order based on the story.

○ ○ ○ ○

| New moon | | | |

○ ○ ○ ○

| | | | |

Moon Phases Adventure

Answer the given questions based on the story "The Mystery of the Moon's Phases"

1. Why do Mia and Leo decide to visit their science teacher?

   _____

   _____

2. How does Mr. Thompson explain the changing shapes of the moon?

   _____

   _____

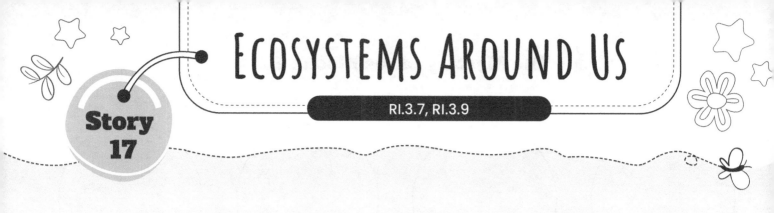

Ecosystems Around Us

RI.3.7, RI.3.9

Story 17

Sara found a special spot outside Willow Creek where many plants and animals lived. It was a hidden place where trees were tall, and a small stream flowed, making beautiful sounds. One day, Sara saw that a part of the stream had dried up, and she knew this was a problem for the plants and animals there.

Wanting to help, Sara looked around carefully. She saw that new buildings were blocking the water from reaching the stream. Sara decided to draw pictures of the place and show how the dried-up stream was bad for the living things there.

She took her drawings to people in the town and explained the problem. Moved by Sara's drawings and her care for the place, the town decided to help. They built a small wall to help some water go back to the dry part of the stream.

Thanks to Sara, the stream flowed again, and the plants and animals were happy. Sara showed everyone how important it is to take care of the places where plants and animals live.

 Sara's Solution Sketch

- Draw a picture of how Sara helped the stream.
- Try to show the new wall and how it helped the water reach the stream.

Two Stories, One Picture

- Look at pictures from "Ecosystems Around Us" and "The Hidden Castle."
- How do the pictures help tell the story of each place?
- What's the same and what's different?

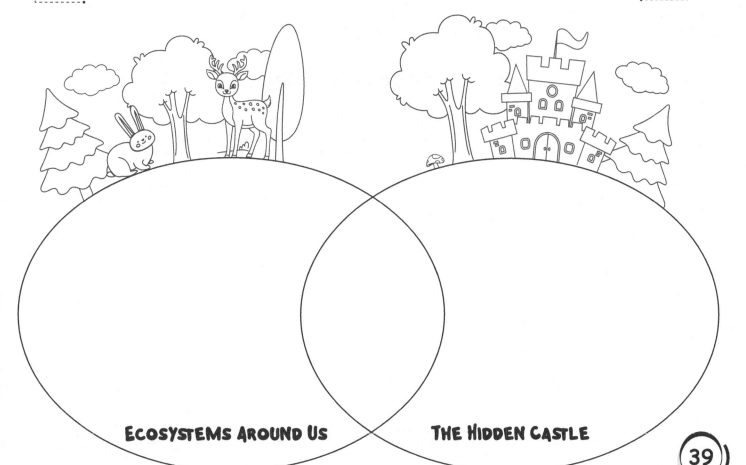

ECOSYSTEMS AROUND US

THE HIDDEN CASTLE

Lily's Lost Teddy

RL.3.7, RL.3.9

Story 18

In the quiet town of Maplewood, Lily had a beloved teddy bear named Mr. Snuggles. One sunny afternoon, while playing in her backyard, Lily noticed Mr. Snuggles was missing. She searched everywhere but couldn't find him. Determined, Lily embarked on a quest throughout Maplewood to find her lost teddy.

Lily visited places she had been with Mr. Snuggles: the park, the library, and the ice cream shop. At each location, she found clues that made her journey even more exciting. Through her adventure, Lily talked to friends and neighbors who joined her search, showing illustrations of Mr. Snuggles and asking if they had seen him.

Finally, at the edge of the park, under the old oak tree, Lily found Mr. Snuggles. He had been there all along, waiting for her return. Lily learned the importance of taking care of her belongings and the value of her community's support.

With Mr. Snuggles back in her arms, Lily felt grateful for the adventure that brought her closer to her friends and neighbors. She realized that every place she visited and every person she talked to was a part of her story with Mr. Snuggles.

 Teddy's Journey Map

- Draw a map of Lily's search for Mr. Snuggles.
- Include the places she visited and the clues she found.
- How do these illustrations help tell the story of her adventure?

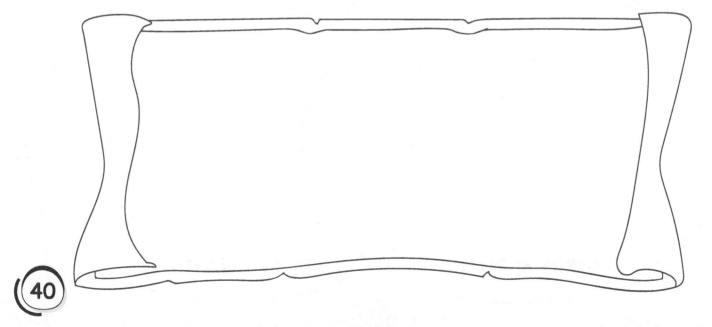

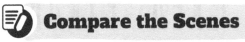

Compare the Scenes

- Look at the two illustrations: one of Lily searching in the park and another in the library.
- Think about how each place is important to Lily's search for Mr. Snuggles.
- Write down how Lily feels in each place and explain how each place helps Lily find Mr. Snuggles.

_____   _____

_____   _____

_____   _____

Then and Now

- Draw your own scene of an adventure with a favorite toy.
- Write a few sentences below the drawing to explain where you are and what you're doing.
- How does your drawing complement the story of Lily and Mr. Snuggles?

_____

The Great Pyramids

RI.3.7, RI.3.9

Story 19

In ancient Egypt, near the busy Nile River, stood the Great Pyramids. Sarah, a curious student from the future, found herself transported back in time by a magical book she found in her attic.

Sarah was amazed by the tall pyramids, busy markets, and beautiful hieroglyphics. Hieroglyphics are a kind of writing used by ancient Egyptians, made up of pictures and symbols. She wanted to learn how the pyramids were built and why.

With the help of Anubis, a young Egyptian boy, and his camel, Zahra, Sarah went on an exciting journey. They met builders, stonecutters, and teachers who shared their knowledge. Sarah learned about the amazing engineering, the hard work of thousands of workers, and the pyramids' importance as tombs for the pharaohs.

One builder told Sarah that the pyramids were made from huge limestone blocks. These blocks were moved across the desert on sleds. The outside of the pyramids was smooth, made from finely cut stones.

Anubis showed Sarah the workers who built the pyramids. They lived in nearby villages and were given food, clothing, and medical care. Building the pyramids was a big team effort that needed careful planning.

Sarah also learned about the Egyptians' beliefs. The pyramids were not just tombs but also believed to be gateways to the afterlife. The Egyptians thought pharaohs became gods after death, and the pyramids helped them on their journey. The pyramids were aligned with the stars, showing the Egyptians' knowledge of the cosmos.

Sarah realized that the pyramids were symbols of the Egyptians' dreams, their understanding of the stars, and their respect for their leaders. She returned to her time, amazed and full of respect for ancient Egyptian civilization.

Pyramid Picture Puzzle

Write down three interesting facts you learned about the pyramids from the story.

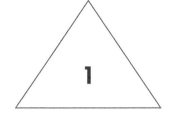

1. _____
2. _____
3. _____

Sarah's Sketchbook

- Imagine you are Sarah, documenting your journey in Egypt.
- Draw a scene from your adventure, focusing on an aspect of the pyramid construction that amazed you the most.
- Write a short caption explaining your drawing.

The Enchanted Forest

Story 20 — RL.3.7, RL.3.9

In the heart of Willowdale, there was a forest known to few as the Enchanted Forest. Mia and her talking dog, Rufus, stumbled upon this magical place one sunny afternoon while chasing a glowing butterfly.

As they ventured deeper, they discovered that the forest was in trouble. A once vibrant and bustling place was wilting because the Magic Crystal that powered the forest's life force had dimmed. Mia and Rufus decided they must help.

Their journey led them to various enchanted beings. First, they met a wise old oak tree who whispered, "Seek the singing frogs by the bubbling brook. They hold a clue." The frogs sang a riddle, hinting, "Find the bear with glasses, for he has the map."

The friendly bear, wearing glasses and reading a book, said, "To recharge the crystal, you must climb to the highest hill. There you will find a dragon who guards it." Each enchanted being shared how the fading magic affected them and offered clues to where the Magic Crystal could be recharged.

Together, Mia and Rufus solved puzzles and overcame challenges, learning about teamwork and the importance of caring for the environment. Finally, they found the Magic Crystal atop the highest hill, guarded by a gentle dragon who was just as worried about the forest.

With a bit of courage and a lot of heart, Mia and Rufus worked with the dragon to recharge the crystal. As its light brightened, the forest sprang back to life, more vibrant than ever.

Returning home, Mia and Rufus knew they had made a difference. The forest was not just a place of magic but a reminder of the magic within each of us to make positive changes in the world.

Forest Friends Gallery

- Draw pictures of the enchanted beings Mia and Rufus met in the forest.
- Next to each drawing, write a sentence about how they help solve the mystery of the dimming Magic Crystal.

Time to Draw!

Create two drawings: one of the Enchanted Forest before Mia and Rufus found the Magic Crystal, and one after it was recharged.

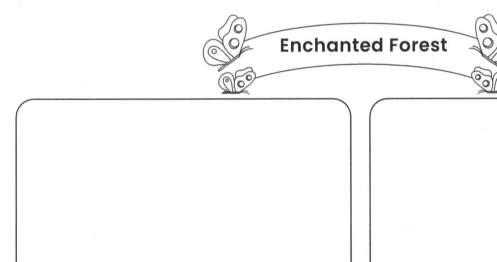

Enchanted Forest

Before

After

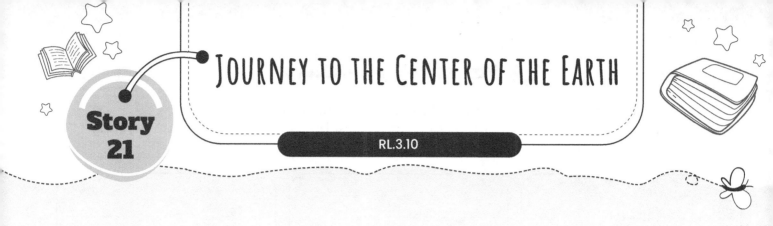

Journey to the Center of the Earth

Story 21 — RL.3.10

In the cozy town of Greenwood, a kid named Alex and their pet lizard, Spike, found an old, dusty book in the attic. This wasn't just any book—it showed a secret path to the center of the Earth! Filled with excitement and eager for an adventure, Alex and Spike decided to see if the map was real.

They found the entrance to the secret path in an old mine in Greenwood, all hidden and tangled in vines. Holding a flashlight and with Spike sitting bravely on their shoulder, Alex started their underground adventure. The walls of the tunnel had puzzles and riddles, and Spike, knowing a lot about rocks and minerals, helped solve them.

As they traveled deeper, they discovered beautiful caves lit by glowing crystals and saw underground rivers as clear as the sky. But then, they came across a huge gap that looked impossible to cross, with the path they needed to follow just on the other side.

Then, Alex had a great idea. They used the crystals to make a bridge across the gap, learning that if you keep trying and use your brain, you can get through tough spots. When they finally got to the center, instead of finding a world of fire, they found a beautiful, green underground world where everything lived in peace.

The journey was incredible, but Alex felt this wonderful place should be kept a secret. So, when they got back home, they hid the book and the entrance to make sure this special underground world stayed safe and secret.

From this adventure, Alex learned that being adventurous means also caring for what you discover, and the best treasures are sometimes those we keep safe for everyone.

 Deep Earth Explorers

Answer questions about Alex and Spike's journey.

1. What challenges did they face, and how did they overcome them?

   _____

   _____

2. Why did Alex decide to keep their discovery a secret?

   _____

   _____

Unwritten Adventures

- Write an additional chapter for the story.
- Imagine Alex and Spike's next adventure.
- Where do they go, and what new mysteries do they uncover?

Amazing Human Body

Story 22

RI.3.10

In the bustling town of Wellville, Jamie discovered a magical microscope that revealed the hidden world inside the human body. Fascinated, Jamie decided to embark on an incredible journey to learn how the body works.

With the help of Dr. Wise, a friendly scientist, and Blinky, a curious cell, Jamie explored the various systems of the body. Their adventure began in the bustling city of the circulatory system, where the Red Blood Cell Road was always busy, transporting oxygen to every part of the body.

Next, they visited the Bone Builders in the skeletal system, learning how bones provide structure and protection. The journey continued to the Brainpower Park in the nervous system, where Jamie saw how the brain sends messages to the body.

However, they encountered a problem in the digestive system, where a group of Nutrient Navigators was lost, unable to find their way to the Small Intestine Street. Jamie, Dr. Wise, and Blinky worked together, guiding the navigators and learning the importance of a balanced diet and exercise.

Their adventure taught Jamie not just about the human body's amazing abilities but also about teamwork and curiosity. Returning to Wellville, Jamie shared these discoveries with friends, inspiring them to take care of their bodies and explore the wonders of science.

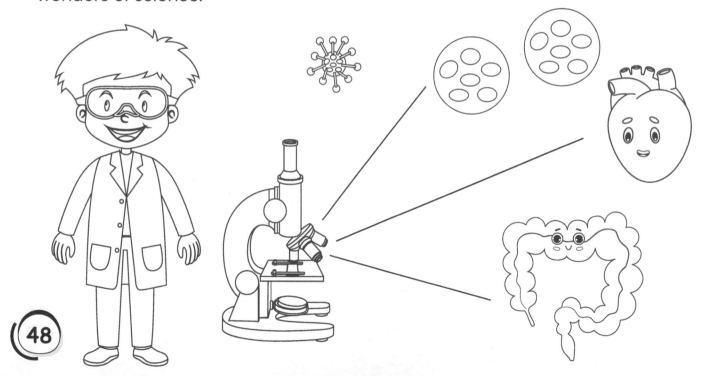

Body System Quest

Answer questions about Jamie's journey.

1. What systems did Jamie explore, and what did they learn in each place?

2. How did solving the problem in the digestive system help Jamie understand the importance of health?

My Body Adventure

- Write a story about your own adventure inside the human body.
- Which system would you visit, and what friends would you make along the way?
- What problem might you solve together?

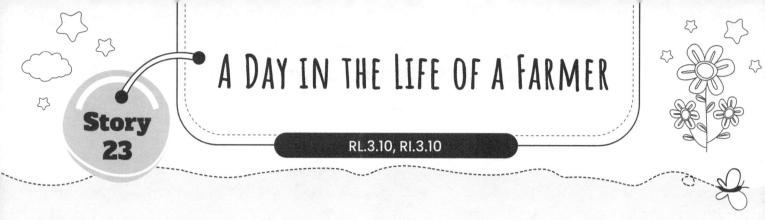

A Day in the Life of a Farmer

Story 23

RL.3.10, RI.3.10

In the lush, green fields of Meadowbrook, young Emma spent her days learning the ropes of farming from her grandmother, Mrs. Willow. One sunny morning, Emma discovered that the scarecrow, which guarded their cornfield, had fallen over during the night. Concerned about the crows, Emma knew she had to act quickly.

With her grandmother's guidance, Emma set out to repair the scarecrow. Along the way, she learned about the different crops they grew and the animals they cared for. She fed the chickens, milked the cows, and even helped plant new seeds in the vegetable garden.

However, fixing the scarecrow proved to be a bigger challenge than she thought. Emma tried various methods, but it kept toppling over. Finally, Mrs. Willow showed her how to secure it firmly in the ground, teaching Emma the value of perseverance and problem-solving.

As the day came to an end, Emma looked out at the thriving farm, feeling a sense of pride and accomplishment. She realized that farming was not just about growing food but about caring for the land and working together to overcome challenges.

❓ Scarecrow Chronicles

Answer questions about Emma's day on the farm.

1. What problems did she face, and how did she solve them?

   _____

   _____

2. What did Emma learn about farming and teamwork?

   _____

   _____

📝 My Farm Adventure

Write a story about your own day on a farm. What tasks would you do? Imagine a problem you might encounter and how you would solve it.

_____

_____

_____

_____

51

History of Computers

Story 24

RI.3.10

In the bustling town of Techville, Alex and Sam discovered an old, dusty computer in their attic. Curious about how it worked, they embarked on a journey through time to learn about the history of computers.

Their first stop was the 1940s, where they met Ada, a brilliant mathematician who introduced them to the first electronic computers. These machines were as big as a room and used mainly during the war to solve complex calculations.

Next, they zoomed to the 1970s, where they encountered Steve, a visionary working in his garage on making computers small enough for people to have in their homes. Alex and Sam were amazed to see the evolution from massive machines to the personal computers we know today.

However, they encountered a problem: the more they learned, the more they realized how much they didn't know. They wondered how computers became so small and powerful.

With the help of their new friends from the past, Alex and Sam discovered the microchip – a tiny device that revolutionized computers, making them faster, smaller, and accessible to everyone.

Returning to the present, Alex and Sam were inspired to share their journey with their classmates, showing how curiosity and innovation have shaped the digital world we live in today.

Journey to the World of Computers

Complete the timeline template with important key events and inventions that Alex and Sam encountered.

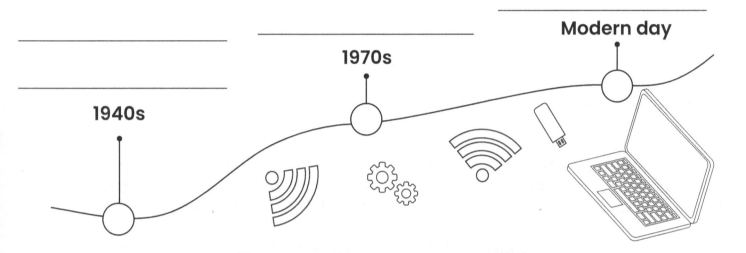

1940s

1970s

Modern day

Invent Your Own Computer

- Imagine you're an inventor creating the next big thing in computers.
- Write a story about your invention, how it works, and how it changes the world.

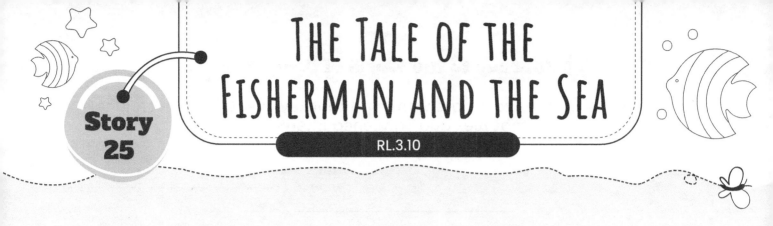

The Tale of the Fisherman and the Sea

Story 25 — RL.3.10

In the serene village of Seabreeze, there lived an old fisherman named Eli. Every morning, Eli set out to sea in his small boat, hoping to catch fish to support his family. But the sea was not generous, and his nets often came back empty.

One day, while casting his net, Eli caught a sparkling, talking fish that pleaded for its life. Moved by the fish's plea, Eli decided to release it back into the sea. In gratitude, the fish offered Eli three wishes. Eli wished for the sea to be abundant with fish, for his village to prosper, and for the health and happiness of his family.

The next morning, Eli found the sea teeming with fish, and his village flourished as never before. But with prosperity came forgetfulness, and the villagers soon took the sea's bounty for granted, neglecting to care for its waters.

Noticing the change, Eli spoke to the sea, apologizing for the villagers' actions and promising to teach them to respect and protect the marine life. The sea listened and continued to provide, as long as the villagers kept their promise.

Through this experience, Eli and the villagers learned the importance of gratitude, stewardship, and living in harmony with nature.

Fisherman's Wishes

Answer questions about the story

a. What were Eli's three wishes?

_____

b. How did Eli's wishes come true?

_____

c. How did the villagers change their behavior towards the sea?

_____

A New Chapter at Sea

Write a story about another adventure Eli has at sea. Perhaps he meets the talking fish again, or discovers a hidden underwater world. What new lessons does he learn?

_____

_____

_____

_____

The Lost Kitten

RL.3.1, RL.3.2, RL.3.4

Story 26

In the quiet town of Maple Grove, Sarah and her brother, Tom, found a small, scared kitten hiding under a bush in their backyard. The kitten, with its fur matted and eyes wide, looked lost and hungry. Sarah and Tom decided they needed to help.

They gently coaxed the kitten out with some milk and a soft blanket. They noticed it had no collar. "We should call her Whiskers until we find her home," Sarah suggested, and Tom agreed.

The next day, they set out to find Whiskers' family, asking neighbors and putting up posters around the town. Despite their efforts, no one claimed the kitten.

During their search, they learned from Mrs. Green, the librarian, that many stray animals were in need of care. Inspired, Sarah and Tom decided to take Whiskers to the vet and officially adopt her.

As Whiskers became part of their family, Sarah and Tom realized the importance of responsibility and compassion. They started volunteering at the local animal shelter, determined to make a difference for other lost pets.

The story concludes with the children understanding that sometimes, helping one small creature can spark a big change, not just in their lives but in their community.

Whiskers' Journey

- Sequence the key events in Whiskers' story from when Sarah and Tom found her to when they decided to adopt her.
- Complete the sequencing map then write a sentence and draw a picture to show the correct order of events from the story.

First   **Next**   **Last**

_____ _____ _____
_____ _____ _____
_____ _____ _____

Finding Whiskers

- Match new words from the story to their definitions.
- Draw a picture that represents each word.

Collar

     A person who works in a library, organizing books and helping people find information.

Librarian

     To offer to do work or help without expecting payment in return.

Volunteering

     A band or strap that goes around the neck of an animal, often used to hold identification tags or to attach a leash.

The First Flight

Story 27

RI.3.1, RI.3.2

In the small, windswept town of Windy Bluff, two young siblings, Mia and Leo, discovered an old, dusty book in their attic titled "The Wonders of Flight." Fascinated by stories of early aviators and their flying machines, they dreamed of soaring through the skies themselves.

Determined to experience flight, Mia and Leo set to work. Using the book as their guide, they gathered materials from around their home and began constructing their own makeshift glider. They encountered many challenges, from finding the right materials to understanding the principles of aerodynamics described in the book.

With perseverance and the help of their inventive grandfather, a retired engineer, Mia and Leo overcame these obstacles. Their grandfather explained the basics of flight and helped them refine their design.

Finally, on a breezy afternoon, with their family and friends cheering them on, Mia and Leo launched their glider from the top of Windy Hill. To their delight and amazement, the glider took off, carrying them briefly through the air before landing safely down the hill.

"The First Flight" was a triumph of imagination, determination, and the joy of discovery. Mia and Leo learned that with curiosity and effort, even the wildest dreams could take flight. They also realized the importance of sharing adventures and successes with those you love.

Glider Blueprint

- Sequence the key steps Mia and Leo took to build their glider.
- Write a sentence and draw a picture to show the correct order of events.

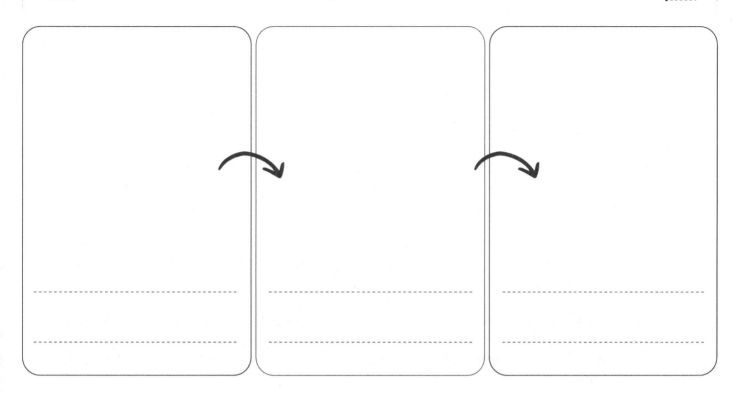

Aviator Vocabulary

- Unscramble each vocabulary word from the story using the hint (definition) provided.
- Write the unscrambled word on the line.

slaemarit
_____ (Hint: The substances or things needed to create something.)

vnieitnve
_____ (Hint: Having the ability to create or design new things.)

wetiswndp
_____ (Hint: Exposed to and swept by the wind.)

roaivat
_____ (Hint: A person who flies aircraft; a pilot.)

dearmde
_____ (Hint: Imagine or desire something that one wants to happen.)

Timmy's Big Day

Story 28 — RL.3.1, RL.3.2

In the vibrant town of Sunnyvale, Timmy, a spirited and curious third grader, woke up feeling excited. Today was the annual Sunnyvale Science Fair, and Timmy had worked hard on his project: a model volcano.

As the fair approached, Timmy encountered a problem. His best friend, Max, who was supposed to bring the baking soda for the volcano eruption, had come down with the flu. Timmy was worried; without the baking soda, his volcano wouldn't erupt.

Determined, Timmy brainstormed solutions. He remembered his science teacher, Mrs. Greene, talking about substitutes for baking soda in experiments. With his mom's help, Timmy found the ingredients needed for the eruption at home.

At the fair, Timmy set up his volcano, explaining his project to the curious onlookers. When it was time for the eruption, Timmy nervously mixed the ingredients. To his delight and the crowd's awe, the volcano erupted spectacularly, earning Timmy a ribbon for creativity and resourcefulness.

Through this experience, Timmy learned the importance of problem-solving, resilience, and the value of knowledge. He realized that even when things don't go as planned, with a little ingenuity and determination, you can still achieve great results.

Plot Elements Definitions

- **Exposition:** The beginning of the story where characters, setting, and the main conflict are introduced.
- **Rising Action:** The series of events that build up to the climax, developing the characters and conflict.
- **Climax:** The turning point of the story, where the main conflict reaches its highest tension.
- **Falling Action:** The events that follow the climax and begin to resolve the conflict.
- **Resolution:** The conclusion of the story, where the conflict is resolved, and the story ends.
- **Theme:** The central message or lesson that the story conveys.

Volcanic Plot Diagram

Briefly describe the events at each part of the plot.

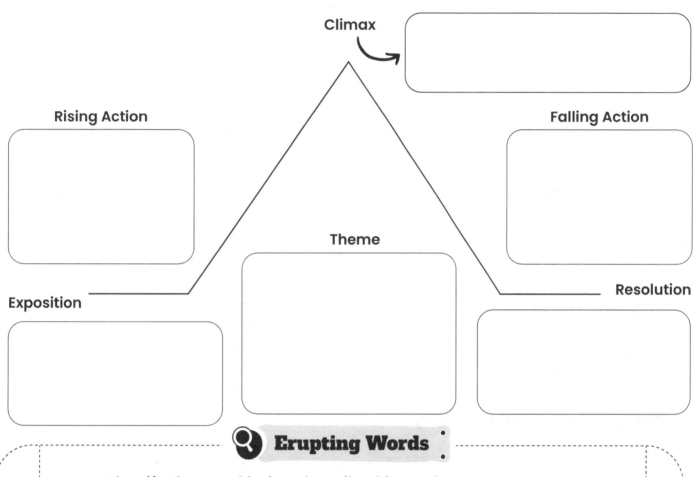

- Climax
- Rising Action
- Falling Action
- Theme
- Exposition
- Resolution

Erupting Words

- Identify the word being described in each sentence.
- Choose your answer from the words listed in the volcano.

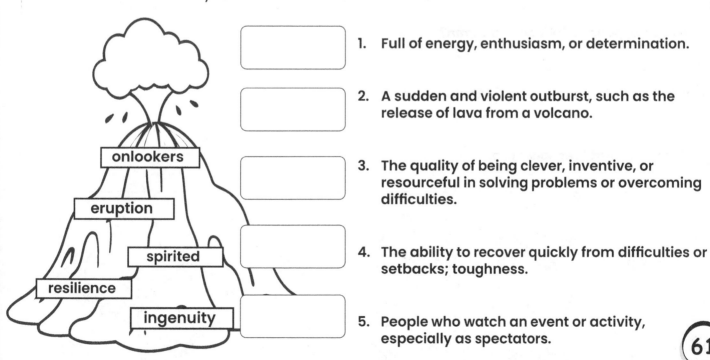

Words in volcano: onlookers, eruption, spirited, resilience, ingenuity

1. Full of energy, enthusiasm, or determination.
2. A sudden and violent outburst, such as the release of lava from a volcano.
3. The quality of being clever, inventive, or resourceful in solving problems or overcoming difficulties.
4. The ability to recover quickly from difficulties or setbacks; toughness.
5. People who watch an event or activity, especially as spectators.

61

The Cycle of Seasons

Story 29

RI.3.1, RI.3.2

In the lively town of Green Meadows, Lily and her friends noticed that the big oak tree in their schoolyard looked different. It was shedding its leaves, preparing for winter. This observation sparked their curiosity about the seasons.

Mrs. Parker, their science teacher, saw this as a perfect opportunity to teach them about the cycle of seasons. She explained how the Earth's tilt and orbit around the sun cause the seasons to change, leading to the variety in weather and nature they observe throughout the year.

To explore this further, Mrs. Parker assigned the class a project to observe and record changes in their environment over the seasons. Lily and her friends decided to focus on the big oak tree.

They took pictures of the tree during each season: its bare branches in winter, budding leaves in spring, full green canopy in summer, and colorful foliage in autumn. They also noted changes in temperature, weather patterns, and animal behavior.

Through this year-long project, Lily and her friends discovered the beauty and consistency of the cycle of seasons. They learned that each season plays a crucial role in the environment, from the rest and renewal in winter to the growth and activity in summer.

Their project concluded with a presentation to the class, sharing their findings and the importance of respecting and protecting nature's cycles. Mrs. Parker praised their effort and creativity, emphasizing how understanding the natural world helps us live in harmony with it.

1. **What does "orbit" mean in the story?**
   _____

2. **Explain "tilt" using an example from the story.**
   _____

3. **What happens to foliage in autumn?**
   _____

4. **What does "renewal" mean in the context of the story?**
   _____

5. **Describe what "seasons" are.**
   _____

Seasonal Snapshots

- Design and color the oak tree according to the sequence of seasons mentioned in the story.
- Describe what happens to the tree in each season.

_____ _____ _____ _____

_____ _____ _____ _____

_____ _____ _____ _____

Weather Words

Tick the checkbox that corresponds to the appropriate definition for each word based on the story.

Orbit:
☐ Spinning around like a top.
☐ The curved path that a planet takes around a star.
☐ How slanted something is.

Renewal:
☐ Fixing something up to make it new again.
☐ Getting more of something that's run out.
☐ Making a paper last longer.

Tilt:
☐ Turning like a merry-go-round.
☐ How much something leans or slopes.
☐ Going around in a circle.

Seasons:
☐ Putting seeds in the ground to grow food.
☐ Special things that happen during different times of the year.
☐ Splitting the year into different weather times.

Foliage:
☐ How leaves are arranged on a plant.
☐ Trees losing their leaves.
☐ Adding stuff to the dirt so plants can grow.

The Secret of the Old Clock

Story 30

RL.3.1, RL.3.2

In the **quaint** town of Maple Ridge, Emma discovered a **mysterious** old clock in her grandmother's attic. Unlike any clock she had seen, it had strange symbols around its face and didn't seem to tell the right time.

Curious, Emma and her best friend, Jake, decided to investigate the clock's history. Their search led them to Mr. Harrison, the town historian, who revealed that the clock was rumored to hold the key to a hidden treasure.

Fueled by excitement, Emma and Jake **embarked** on a **quest** to decipher the **symbols**. Along the way, they learned about the town's history, solved puzzles, and uncovered clues hidden in landmarks they had passed by countless times.

Their journey wasn't without challenges. They had to compare their findings, debate their next steps, and learn to trust their instincts. The symbols, they discovered, represented important dates in the town's history, which guided them to the treasure's location.

In the end, the treasure they found wasn't gold or jewels but a collection of historical artifacts that told the story of Maple Ridge's founding families. Emma and Jake decided to donate the collection to the local museum, earning praise for their dedication and teamwork.

The adventure brought the community together, with Emma and Jake at the heart of it, proving that curiosity, courage, and collaboration can uncover the most valuable treasures.

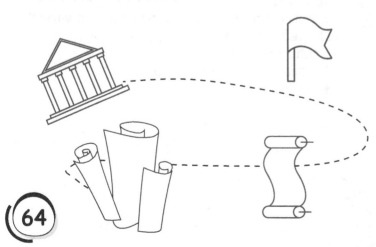

Clockwork Adventure

After reading the story, answer the given questions below.

What was the main idea of the story?

_____

_____

List three key events or actions that support the main idea.

_____

_____

_____

What lessons can be learned from Emma and Jake's adventure?

_____

_____

Deciphering the Past

- Read the story carefully and identify the vocabulary words in bold.
- Use the context of the story to help you understand and define the words.

1) Quaint
In the story, Maple Ridge is described as a quaint town. Based on how the town is described, what do you think "quaint" means?

_____

2) Mysterious
Emma found a mysterious old clock. What about the clock makes it mysterious?

_____

3) Symbols
The clock had strange symbols around its face. What do you think these symbols represent?

_____

4) Embarked
Based on Jake and Emma's adventure, what do you think "embarked" means?

_____

5) Quest
Based on Jake and Emma's adventure, what do you think a "quest" is?

_____

The Invisible Dragon

Story 31 — RL.3.3, RL.3.4

In the mystical village of Whispering Woods, there lived a young girl named Ellie who had the rare ability to see dragons. One day, she encountered an invisible dragon named Whispy, who was misunderstood by the villagers because they could not see or understand him.

Whispy felt lonely and often accidentally caused trouble, trying to interact with the villagers who were scared of things they didn't understand. Ellie, understanding Whispy's loneliness, decided to help him find a way to communicate and live peacefully with the villagers.

Ellie and Whispy worked together, doing kind deeds around the village, like fetching water and helping the crops grow. Slowly, the villagers started noticing these good deeds and wondered who was behind them.

Despite this, the villagers were still afraid of Whispy. Ellie came up with a plan to show everyone Whispy's true nature. She organized a village meeting and, using a special flower that could make invisible things visible, she introduced Whispy to everyone.

The villagers were amazed to see Whispy and learned that he only wanted to be friends. Although Whispy's visibility was temporary, the impact was lasting. The villagers learned to appreciate the unseen, and Whispy felt accepted and happy.

Ellie and Whispy's story taught the village that just because you can't see something doesn't mean it's not there or doesn't matter. They learned the importance of understanding and accepting differences.

Mapping Whispy's Journey

Use the information from the story to fill in each section of the character map.

Whispy's Traits

Whispy's Deeds

Whispy

How Ellie influenced the villagers' perception of Whispy

Lessons learned by the village from Whispy's story

Different Perspectives

- Complete the table below. Discuss how different characters might have viewed Whispy's actions differently before knowing who he was.
- Focus on a specific event and show different viewpoints.

Character	Point of View

Journey through the Human Body

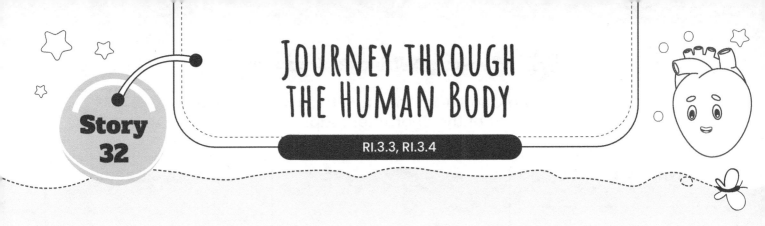

In the town of Cellville, Mia and her microscopic friends embarked on an extraordinary journey through the human body. Their mission was to learn how different parts work together to keep the body healthy.

Their first stop was the bustling Brain Central, where they met Neuron Nate, who explained how he sends messages to the body. "Without us, you couldn't even move a muscle!" he boasted, showing them the lightning-fast network of communication.

Next, they dived into the Heart Harbor, where Cardio Carl, a strong and steady heart cell, showed them how he pumps blood. "We're like the delivery service," Carl explained, "bringing oxygen and nutrients to every part."

The journey continued through the Lungs Lookout with Breezy Bella, who shared how she helps bring oxygen into the body. "It's all about the breath of life!" Bella exclaimed as they watched air flow in and out.

However, not all was well in Cellville. They encountered areas where germs were causing trouble. Together, Mia and her friends learned about the immune system's defenders, led by Immuno Izzy, who fought off the invaders to keep the body healthy.

Their adventure highlighted the importance of teamwork, healthy habits, and the marvels of the human body. Mia realized that every cell has a critical role, and by working together, they ensure the body's wellbeing.

Upon returning, Mia shared her newfound knowledge with her class, inspiring them to appreciate and take care of their bodies.

Mapping Mia's Micro-Adventure

Create a character map for Mia and for the other characters in the story.
- ◇ Identify each character's role in the story.
- ◇ Describe the key traits of each character.

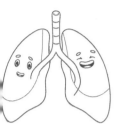

Mia

Role: _____

Key traits: _____

_____

Neuron Nate

Role: _____

Key traits: _____

_____

Cardio Carl

Role: _____

Key traits: _____

_____

Breezy Bella

Role: _____

Key traits: _____

_____

Immuno Izzy

Role: _____

Key traits: _____

_____

Different Perspectives

- ◇ Create a comic strip showing how Neuron Nate, Cardio Carl, and Breezy Bella might view their importance to the body differently.
- ◇ Use dialogue examples from the story.

The Mermaid's Adventure

Story 33

RL.3.3, RL.3.4

In the underwater kingdom of Aquaria, Marina, a young mermaid with a curious heart, discovered a mysterious coral reef she had never seen before. Hidden within the reef was a magical pearl that glowed with an enchanting light.

Marina learned from her grandmother, Pearl, that the pearl held the power to purify the ocean waters but had been lost for centuries. Motivated by a desire to help her ocean friends and restore the beauty of Aquaria, Marina embarked on a quest to activate the pearl's power.

Her journey was filled with challenges. She encountered sea creatures in need and helped them, earning their trust and friendship. Among them were Coral, a wise turtle who taught Marina the importance of patience, and Fin, a playful dolphin who reminded her to enjoy the journey.

The main problem started when a big storm scattered the pieces of the magical pearl all over the ocean. Marina, with the help of her new friends, set out to find and reassemble the pearl.

Through teamwork and determination, Marina and her friends overcame obstacles, from deep-sea currents to encounters with mysterious sea creatures. Each piece of the pearl they found brought them closer to their goal, teaching Marina valuable lessons about courage, friendship, and the power of working together.

In the end, Marina successfully reassembled the pearl, purifying the waters of Aquaria. The ocean once again thrived, filled with vibrant life and color. Marina's adventure showed her that even the smallest mermaid could make a big difference with a kind heart and a brave spirit.

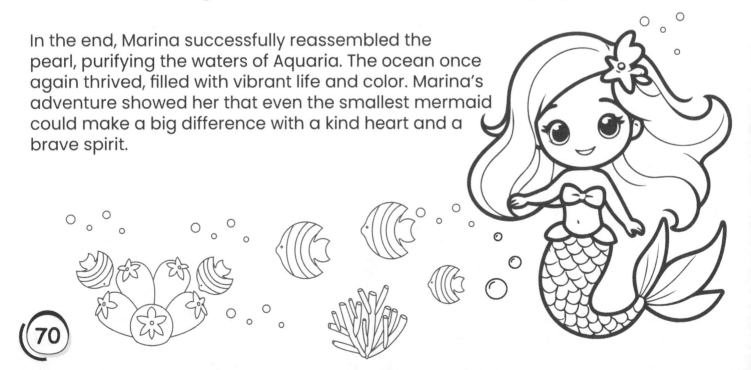

Marina's Journey Map

- Complete the character map below.
- Draw the character of Marina and list her traits, motivations, and how she interacts with other characters throughout her adventure.

Character's Trait

Character's Feelings

Character's Conflict

Character's Solution

Character's Name

Viewpoints Under the Sea

- Discuss how different characters, like Coral the turtle and Fin the dolphin, might view the same event differently.
- Choose a specific event from the story for discussion.

_____
_____
_____
_____
_____
_____

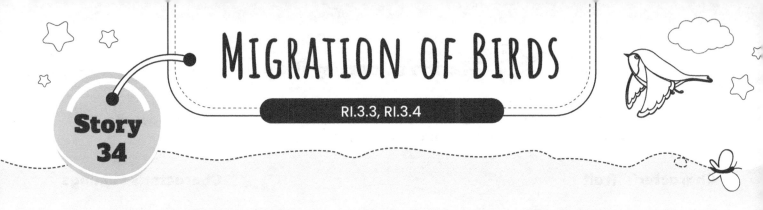

Migration of Birds

RI.3.3, RI.3.4

Story 34

In the vibrant forest of Greenwood, a curious young robin named Ruby wanted to learn why birds migrate. She observed many of her friends preparing for a long journey southward as winter approached, but she didn't understand why.

Ruby decided to ask her elders and friends about migration. Her first stop was Oliver, the wise old owl, who explained, "Migration is a journey we take to find warmer places with more food during winter."

But Ruby was still curious about how they knew where to go. She flew to meet Sophia, the swift sparrow, who shared, "We follow the stars and the landscapes below. It's a knowledge passed down to us."

As the day of departure neared, Ruby felt nervous but excited. She joined her family and friends on their first migration journey. Along the way, she experienced the challenges and beauties of the journey, including flying over majestic mountains and vast lakes.

The most critical moment came when a storm separated Ruby from her group. Using the stars and landmarks as Sophia taught her, Ruby bravely navigated through the storm and reunited with her group, realizing the strength and courage she possessed.

Upon reaching their destination, Ruby felt a sense of accomplishment and understood the importance of migration for survival. She looked forward to sharing her newfound knowledge and experiences with others.

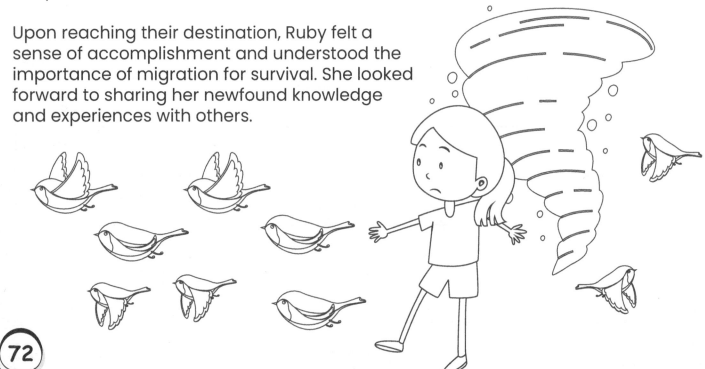

Ruby's Flight Path

- Complete the Character Development Map for Ruby, detailing her traits, motivations, and how she grows throughout her migration journey.
- Include how her interactions with Oliver and Sophia contribute to her understanding and courage.

BEFORE

How the character feels

How the character acts

CHARACTER

Cause
What caused this character to change during the story?

AFTER

How the character feels

How the character acts

Different Feathers, Different Views

- Create a comic strip showing how Ruby, Oliver, and Sophia might view the migration differently.
- Focus on their unique perspectives based on their experiences and knowledge.

The Brave Little Soldier

Story 35 — RL.3.3, RL.3.4

In the peaceful land of Meadowfield, there lived a toy soldier named Tim. Despite being the smallest soldier in the toy box, Tim had the biggest heart and dreamed of leading grand adventures and protecting the kingdom.

One night, a mischievous cat knocked the toy box over, scattering the toys across the room. Tim found himself under the bed, far from his fellow soldiers. Determined to reunite with them, Tim embarked on a perilous journey across the vast bedroom terrain.

Along the way, Tim encountered various obstacles: a steep mountain of books, a wide river of spilled water, and a dark forest of chair legs. Despite these challenges, Tim's courage never wavered. He used his wits to navigate each obstacle, learning valuable lessons from each encounter.

His greatest challenge came when he stumbled upon a lost teddy bear, Bella, who was afraid of the dark. Remembering how he felt under the bed, Tim vowed to help Bella find her way back to the toy shelf. Together, they faced their fears and discovered the strength of friendship.

Upon reaching the toy shelf, Tim and Bella were greeted with cheers. Tim had not only found his way back but had also brought a new friend. The toys celebrated Tim's bravery and welcomed Bella into their fold.

Tim realized that being brave didn't mean going on grand adventures; it meant standing up for others and being a friend. He had become the leader he always wanted to be, not through size, but through the courage of his heart.

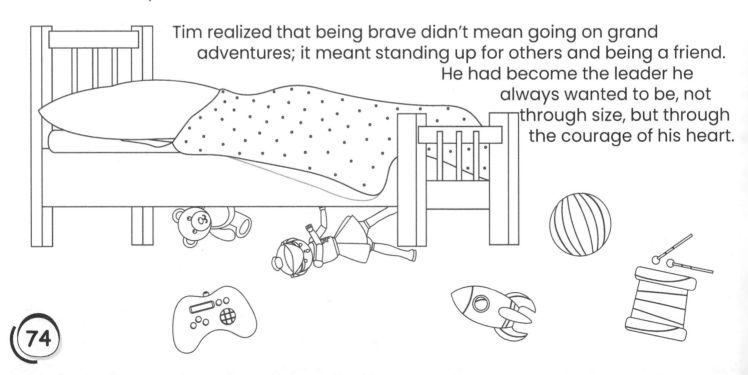

Tim's Heroic Path

- Accomplish the character map for Tim, showing his journey, the challenges he faced, his solutions, and how he grew as a character.
- Include his interactions with Bella and the lessons learned.

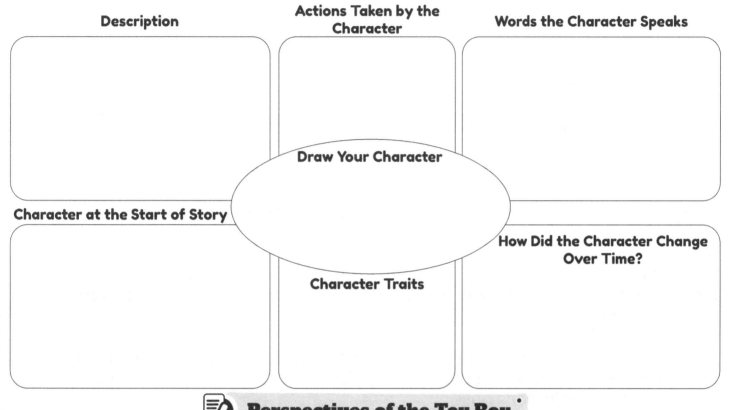

Perspectives of the Toy Box

- Discuss how Tim's adventure might be viewed differently by the other toys and Bella.
- Consider their feelings before and after the adventure.

Point of View (POV)

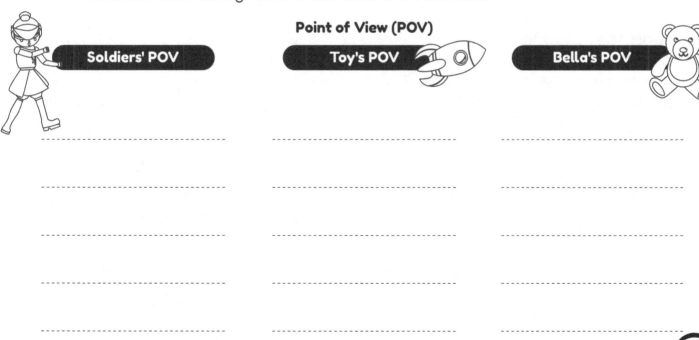

The Treasure Hunt

RL.3.5, RL.3.6

In the bustling town of Cove Harbor, four friends—Lucas, Emma, Aiden, and Zoe—discovered an old map in Lucas's attic, hidden within an ancient book of pirate tales. The map hinted at a hidden treasure buried somewhere in the town, left behind by the legendary pirate Captain Redbeard.

Eager to find the treasure, the friends set out on an adventure, each bringing their unique skills to the team. Lucas was the leader, Emma had a knack for solving riddles, Aiden was a history buff, and Zoe was brave and loved exploring.

Their quest was filled with challenges. The map led them to various historical landmarks in Cove Harbor, each clue intricately linked to the next. Along the way, they encountered cryptic riddles, secret passages, and even rumors of a ghost guarding the treasure.

As they pieced together the clues, they learned that the treasure wasn't gold or jewels but a time capsule left by the town's founders, containing artifacts and stories from Cove Harbor's past.

In their journey, the friends not only uncovered the town's history but also learned valuable lessons about teamwork, perseverance, and the real treasure of friendship.

In the end, they decided to add their own stories and artifacts to the time capsule before re-burying it for future adventurers to find, continuing the legacy of discovery and friendship.

Viewpoints of Adventure

- Discuss how the story changes when told from the perspective of Lucas, Emma, Aiden, or Zoe.
- Focus on a specific event, like finding the first clue or solving a riddle, and explore how each character's strengths and fears might influence their viewpoint.

Mapping the Hunt

- Outline the treasure hunt's story structure, including the sequence of clues and landmarks the friends visit.
- Use illustrations or bullet points to show any flashbacks or time jumps that enrich the narrative.

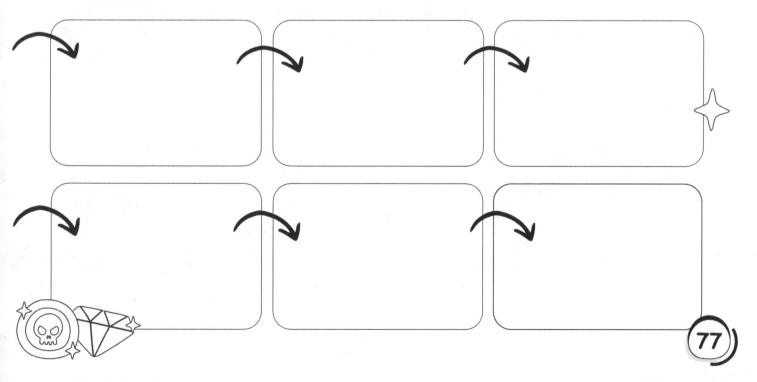

Life in the Ocean

Story 37 — RI.3.5, RI.3.6

In the vast, shimmering world beneath the waves of the Pacific Ocean, a young dolphin named Fin embarked on a journey to discover the secrets of the ocean. Fin was fascinated by stories of hidden underwater cities and mysterious creatures told by his grandmother, Coral.

One day, Fin decided it was time to explore these wonders himself. His first encounter was with Shelly, a wise old turtle, who shared tales of ancient ruins hidden deep in the Mariana Trench. Inspired, Fin swam deeper, guided by the light of glowing jellyfish.

As he swam deeper into the ocean, Fin met different sea animals. Each offered different perspectives on ocean life. He met a school of fish that moved together as one to escape predators, a solitary octopus who camouflaged itself in coral gardens, and a majestic whale who spoke of the ocean's vastness and its need for protection.

The central problem Fin observed was the pollution affecting his new friends' homes. Determined to help, Fin rallied the ocean creatures to gather the debris and clean their home. Along the way, Fin learned the importance of teamwork, courage, and taking care of the environment.

In the end, Fin returned home, not with tales of hidden cities, but with a story of how even the smallest creature can make a big difference. He realized that the true secret of the ocean was its resilience and the collective strength of its inhabitants.

Fin's Ocean Friends

Create a character map for Fin and the creatures he meets, exploring their motivations and how they contribute to the ocean's ecosystem and the story's events.

Different Waves, Different Tales

- Explore how the story changes when told from the viewpoints of Shelly the turtle, the school of fish, the octopus, and the whale.
- Discuss how each character's unique experiences and challenges shape their perspective on ocean life.

Character's name: _____

Viewpoint: _____

_____

_____

Character's name: _____

Viewpoint: _____

_____

_____

Character's name: _____

Viewpoint: _____

_____

_____

Character's name: _____

Viewpoint: _____

_____

_____

The Giant's Secret

RL.3.5, RL.3.6

Story 38

In the serene village of Willowbrook, nestled at the foot of the Whispering Mountains, the villagers whispered tales of a gentle giant named Gulliver, who lived hidden in the forest. Despite his intimidating size, Gulliver had a heart of gold and a love for all creatures, big and small.

The story begins when Mia, a curious and brave young girl from the village, stumbled upon Gulliver while exploring the forest. Unlike her fellow villagers, Mia saw past Gulliver's towering presence and discovered his secret: Gulliver had the magical ability to speak with animals and heal them with his touch.

Gulliver shared with Mia that he stayed hidden because he feared his powers might scare the villagers or be misunderstood. Mia, moved by Gulliver's kindness and his special bond with the forest animals, promised to keep his secret.

However, when a mysterious illness spread through the village's livestock, Mia knew that Gulliver's healing abilities could save them. Faced with a difficult decision, Mia convinced Gulliver to help, promising to help him reveal his secret on his terms.

Together, they cured the animals, and Mia helped the villagers see the gentle giant for who he truly was, not just a creature of legend but a friend and protector of Willowbrook. Gulliver was welcomed into the village, and the story ends with a celebration of newfound friendship and unity between the villagers and Gulliver.

Gulliver's World: A Different View

- Explore the narrative from the viewpoints of Mia, Gulliver, and the villagers.
- Discuss how the story changes based on who's telling it, especially focusing on the discovery of Gulliver's secret and the village crisis.

_____

_____

_____

_____

_____

_____

The Sequence of Secrets

- Fill in the map below by drawing events in the order they happened.
- Describe each event by filling in the blanks under each drawing.

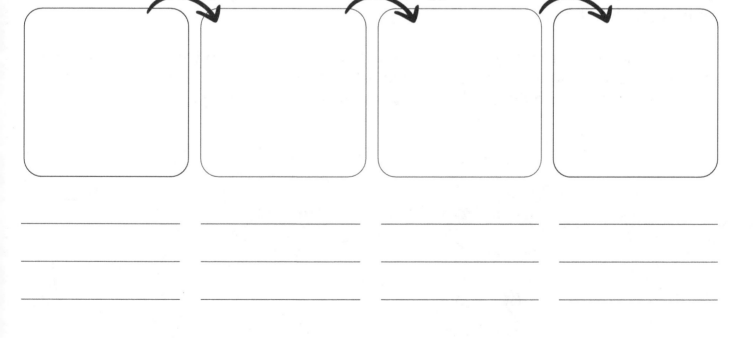

Wonders of the Rainforest

Story 39 — RI.3.5, RI.3.6

In the heart of the vibrant Amazon Rainforest, Maya, a young explorer, embarked on a journey to discover its wonders. Accompanied by her parrot friend, Rico, Maya was eager to learn about the rainforest's secrets and the diverse life it harbored.

Their adventure began at the break of dawn, with the forest awakening to the symphony of wildlife. Maya and Rico met various inhabitants of the rainforest, each sharing their unique story and perspective on life in this lush paradise.

First, they encountered Leo, the wise old jaguar, who spoke of the rainforest's ancient trees and the importance of preserving their home. Next, they met Bella, the butterfly, who described the beauty of transformation and the interconnectedness of all living things.

As Maya and Rico ventured deeper, they discovered a hidden waterfall, a sight so breathtaking it seemed like a secret world. However, they also saw signs of danger—areas where the forest was threatened by deforestation and loss of habitat.

Determined to make a difference, Maya decided to document their discoveries and the stories of their new friends, hoping to share the beauty and importance of the rainforest with the world.

Their journey was a testament to the resilience of nature and the urgent need for conservation. In the end, Maya and Rico returned home, their hearts filled with hope and a renewed commitment to protect the Amazon Rainforest.

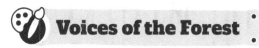
Voices of the Forest

- Explore the narrative from the viewpoints of Maya, Rico, Leo the jaguar, and Bella the butterfly.
- Discuss how each character's experiences and insights contribute to the story's message about conservation and biodiversity.

Character: _____

Character: _____

Character: _____

Character: _____

Time to Draw!

- Inside each box is one of the key events from Maya and Rico's exploration.
- Arrange the events of the story in proper sequence by numbering them as 1-5.

They discover a hidden waterfall, but also witness signs of danger due to deforestation.

They encounter Leo, the wise old jaguar, who speaks about the importance of preserving the rainforest.

Maya decides to document their discoveries and stories of their new friends, aiming to share the importance of the rainforest with the world.

Maya and Rico begin their journey at dawn, meeting various inhabitants of the rainforest.

Maya and Rico meet Bella, the butterfly, who describes the beauty of transformation and interconnectedness.

The Mystery of the Missing Crown

Story 40 — RL.3.5, RL.3.6

In the peaceful kingdom of Greenwood, the royal crown went missing just days before the grand coronation of Prince Elliot. The entire kingdom was in a state of worry, and a young detective named Lucy was called upon to solve the mystery.

Lucy, known for her sharp wit and keen observation skills, began her investigation by interviewing the castle's inhabitants, from the royal guards to the kitchen staff. Each character provided a different viewpoint on the day the crown disappeared, revealing a complex web of stories and alibis.

As Lucy pieced together the sequence of events, she discovered that the crown was not stolen out of malice but accidentally misplaced by Sir Whiskers, the castle cat, who had been playing in the treasury room.

The central problem was not only finding the missing crown but also understanding the perspectives and actions of those involved. Lucy's investigation highlighted themes of misunderstanding, responsibility, and the importance of communication.

With the mystery solved, the crown was found in a stack of linen in the laundry room, exactly where Sir Whiskers had left it. Prince Elliot's coronation proceeded with great celebration, and Lucy was hailed as a hero.

The story concluded with Lucy reflecting on her adventure, realizing that every mystery has multiple viewpoints and that the truth often lies in understanding them all.

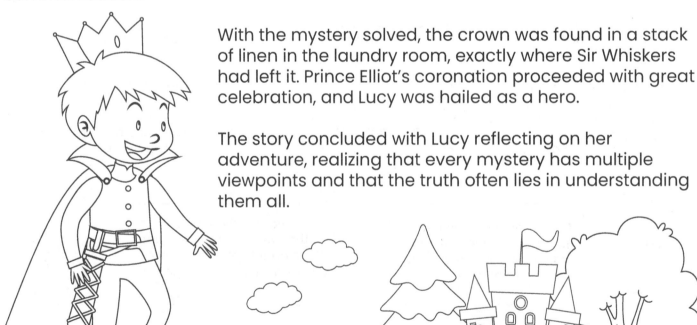

Detective's Diary

- Write diary entries from Lucy, Sir Whiskers, and Prince Elliot's perspectives about the day the crown went missing.
- Discuss how each character's viewpoint provides different insights into the mystery.

Time to Draw!

Create a visual timeline of the events leading up to the discovery of the missing crown, including any flashbacks or time jumps that Lucy uncovers during her investigation.

The Magical Door

RL.3.7, RL.3.9

Story 41

In the small town of Evergreen, nestled between rolling hills and whispering forests, there stood an ancient library, home to a magical door that was hidden from the eyes of those who did not believe in magic. Sarah, a curious and adventurous third grader, stumbled upon this secret door while searching for a book on her favorite topic: dragons.

The door was ornately carved with symbols of mythical creatures and shimmered with an ethereal glow. Sarah, with her heart pounding with excitement and hands trembling with anticipation, pushed the door open and stepped into a world beyond her wildest dreams.

She found herself in the Land of Fantasia, where dragons soared in the skies, unicorns roamed the meadows, and talking animals shared stories of ancient magic. Here, Sarah embarked on a quest to find the Crystal of Wisdom, the source of Fantasia's magic, which had been stolen by a mischievous goblin.

With the help of her new friends—a wise owl named Oliver, a brave unicorn named Luna, and a friendly dragon named Ember—Sarah navigated through enchanted forests, crossed mystical rivers, and climbed the tallest mountains.

Through her journey, Sarah discovered that the true magic lay not just in the land around her but within herself. Her courage, kindness, and unwavering belief in magic were the keys to overcoming challenges and unlocking the mysteries of Fantasia.

In the end, Sarah and her friends retrieved the Crystal of Wisdom, restoring magic to Fantasia. As she returned to the library through the magical door, Sarah realized that her adventure had just begun. Every book was a doorway to a new world, waiting to be explored.

Fantasia Through My Eyes

- Draw a scene from Sarah's adventure in Fantasia using details from the story.
- Focus on how the illustrations can add depth and emotion to the narrative.

Two Worlds Collide

- Compare and contrast the illustrations and text from "The Magical Door" with another story.
- Discuss how each set complements the other and enhances the storytelling.

The Magical Door | **Chosen Story**

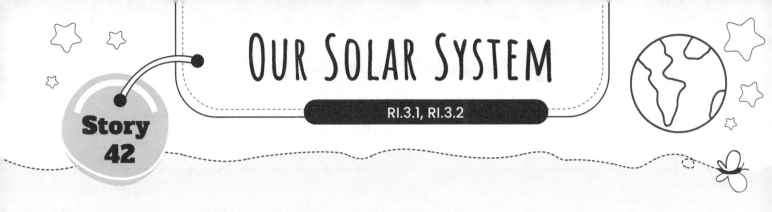

Our Solar System

Story 42 — RI.3.1, RI.3.2

Lucy and Max, two inquisitive third graders, embark on an imaginary journey through our solar system, guided by their science book and a sprinkle of magic. Their bedroom transforms into a spaceship, and each planet they visit comes alive from the pages of their book.

First, they zoom past Mercury, feeling the heat from its close proximity to the Sun. Venus, shrouded in thick clouds, reveals secrets of its scorching surface. Earth greets them with familiar blues and greens, while Mars shows off its towering volcanoes and grand canyons.

Jupiter's swirling storms fascinate them, especially the Great Red Spot. Saturn's rings, made of ice and rock, sparkle like jewels. Uranus surprises them with its tilted axis, and Neptune enchants with its deep blue hue.

Along their journey, Lucy and Max learn not just about the planets, but also about the importance of exploration, curiosity, and caring for our own planet, Earth. Their adventure concludes with a newfound appreciation for the vastness and beauty of the solar system and a commitment to being young stewards of Earth.

Planetary Portraits

- Draw your favorite scene from Lucy and Max's journey, focusing on how the illustrations of planets can enhance the story.
- Use vibrant colors and details to bring the scene to life.

Two Tales of the Cosmos

- Compare the illustrations and text from "Our Solar System" with Story 5 "Starstruck".
- Discuss how each set of illustrations complements its story and the differences in how they present space exploration.

The Secret Garden

RI.3.7, RI.3.9

Story 43

Emma, a curious and adventurous third-grader, discovers a hidden door in the old wall of her grandmother's garden during a summer visit. Behind the door, she finds a neglected garden, overgrown and seemingly forgotten by time. Emma decides to bring the garden back to life.

With the help of her friend Jacob and her grandmother, who shares stories of the garden's past glory, Emma begins the task of clearing, planting, and nurturing. As the garden transforms, so does Emma's understanding of friendship, family, and the importance of caring for the environment.

Together, they uncover the garden's secrets, including a magical tree that blooms with flowers of every color imaginable, attracting butterflies and birds that had once vanished from the area. The garden becomes a place of wonder and beauty, a haven for wildlife, and a gathering spot for the community.

The story concludes with the garden in full bloom, a symbol of renewal and hope, teaching Emma and her friends about the power of collaboration, perseverance, and the magic hidden in the natural world.

Illustrate the Transformation

- Draw a before and after scene of the secret garden based on Emma's restoration efforts.
- Focus on how the illustrations can show the change over time and enhance the narrative.

Gardens of Stories

- Compare the illustrations and text from "The Secret Garden" with Story 25: "The Tale of the Fisherman and the Sea".
- Discuss how each set of illustrations complements its story and what differences in themes are highlighted through the imagery.

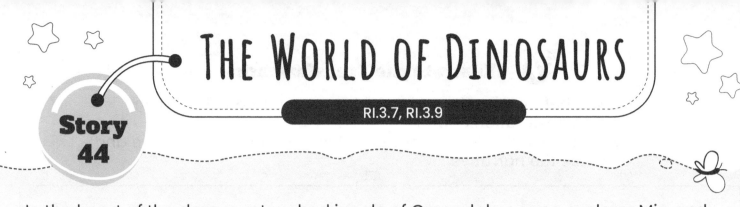

The World of Dinosaurs

Story 44

RI.3.7, RI.3.9

In the heart of the dense, untouched jungle of Greendale, young explorer Mia and her scientist friend Alex discover a hidden valley that time forgot, home to living dinosaurs! With sketchbooks in hand, they embark on an extraordinary journey to document these magnificent creatures.

Their first encounter is with a gentle Triceratops, munching on ferns. Mia sketches quickly, capturing its massive body and three fierce horns. Next, they hide as a T-Rex thunders by, its mighty roar echoing. Alex notes its towering height and sharp teeth, whispering facts to Mia as she draws.

Venturing further, they marvel at a herd of Brachiosaurus, their long necks reaching high into the treetops. They witness a pack of Velociraptors coordinating in a hunt, showcasing their intelligence and speed.

As the sun sets, they find a secluded spot by a crystal-clear lake, watching Pterosaurs glide above and Stegosaurus wade through the water. Mia and Alex discuss how these creatures have survived, a secret valley untouched by time.

Returning home, their sketches and notes become a mini-exhibition at school, sharing their discovery (kept secret to protect the dinosaurs) and educating their peers about these ancient giants. They talk about the importance of preserving such wonders, both past and present.

Dinosaur Discovery Drawing

- Look at the pictures of different dinosaurs Mia and Alex saw.
- Compare and contrast these dinosaurs based on their appearance, behavior, and size.

Dinosaur	Appearance	Behavior	Size
Triceratops			
T-Rex			
Brachiosaurus			
Pterosaur			

Which dinosaur would you want to encounter? Why?

Prehistoric Perspectives

- Compare the illustrations and descriptions from "The World of Dinosaurs" with another dinosaur story.
- Discuss how different illustrations can change our understanding and feelings about these ancient creatures.

The Three Wishes

Story 45

RL.3.7, RL.3.9

In the small town of Greenwood, Mia and her best friend Leo find an ancient, shimmering coin in the creek behind their school. When they clean it, a genie named Zara appears, offering them three wishes.

Their first wish is for the ultimate ice cream sundae, which appears instantly, making them giggle with delight. For their second wish, they ask for the ability to fly, and Zara grants it, leading them on a breathtaking flight around their town.

However, for their third wish, Mia and Leo reflect on what they truly desire. After witnessing a local shelter struggling to care for its animals, they wish for the shelter to have all the resources it needs. Zara smiles, and with a wave of her hand, the shelter is transformed into a paradise for the animals.

In the end, Mia and Leo learn the value of kindness and thinking of others. They promise to keep Zara's secret and to always remember the adventure they shared.

 Magical Moments

Draw one of the wishes Mia and Leo made come to life. Focus on how your illustration captures the magic and emotion of the moment.

A Tale of Two Stories

- Compare "The Three Wishes" with the famous story "Aladdin".
- Discuss how the illustrations and text from both stories help convey their messages and themes.

Comparing Two Stories

	The Three Wishes	Aladdin
Characters		
Setting		
Plot		

Wishing Well

1) How did Mia and Leo show generosity in the story?

_____
_____

2) How did the wishes help them show friendship?

_____
_____

3) Why is it important to make thoughtful wishes?

_____
_____

The City of Gold

RL.3.10

Story 46

In a lush, hidden valley surrounded by towering mountains, lay a city glittering with gold. This city, unseen by modern eyes, was home to a friendly community of animals who could speak like humans. Among them was Leo, a young, adventurous lion, and his best friend, Ellie, a wise elephant.

One day, a map landed at their feet, carried by the wind. It was a map to a hidden part of the city, where the greatest treasure was said to be hidden. Filled with excitement, Leo and Ellie decided to follow the map.

Their journey was filled with puzzles and riddles, testing their wit and bravery. They helped each other, combining Leo's courage with Ellie's wisdom. After crossing rivers, mountains, and forests, they finally found the treasure - a library filled with ancient books.

Leo and Ellie realized that the true treasure was not gold but knowledge. They shared their discovery with their friends, turning the library into a place of learning for all. The city glowed brighter than ever, enriched by the treasure of wisdom.

Quest for Knowledge

After reading "The City of Gold," answer questions about the story.

A What kind of animals lived in the hidden valley city?
_____

B How did Leo and Ellie find out about the hidden treasure?
_____

C What were some challenges Leo and Ellie faced on their journey to find the treasure?
_____

D What did Leo and Ellie find at the end of their journey?
_____

E What did Leo and Ellie realize was the true treasure in the end?
_____

Create Your Adventure

- Imagine finding a map to another part of the City of Gold.
- Write a story about what you find there. Use elements like friendship, bravery, and discovery.

_____
_____
_____
_____
_____

The Evolution of Technology

RI.3.10

In the bustling town of Innovatia, nestled between rolling hills and sparkling streams, lived Timmy, a curious third grader with a fascination for gadgets and gizmos. One sunny afternoon, while exploring his grandpa's attic, Timmy stumbled upon a dusty, old book titled "The Evolution of Technology."

With wide eyes, Timmy flipped through the pages, discovering stories of the first computers that were as big as a room, to the invention of the internet, connecting people across the globe, and finally, to the latest in virtual reality that could transport you to different worlds. Each page was a new adventure, showing how inventions changed lives and shaped the future.

Determined to share these wonders, Timmy decided to create a mini-museum at school, displaying models of inventions mentioned in the book. With help from his friends, they crafted everything from cardboard computers to paper smartphones, each accompanied by a short history Timmy had learned.

The day of the presentation, Timmy explained how technology evolved, highlighting how creativity and perseverance led to innovations that made life easier and more fun. His classmates were amazed, and the mini-museum became a hit, inspiring everyone to imagine and invent.

Through "The Evolution of Technology," Timmy and his friends learned that technology was more than just gadgets; it was a story of human achievement and endless possibilities.

Tech Time Travel

- Draw your favorite invention mentioned in the story.
- Imagine how it might change in the future and draw that too!

Then and Now

- Choose two technologies from the story.
- Write about how each one was used in the past and how it is used now.

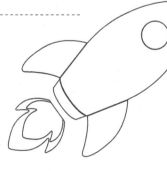

The Cursed Pirate Ship

RL.3.10, RI.3.10

Story 48

In the small coastal village of Seabreeze, tales of a cursed pirate ship, The Phantom Wave, whispered through the streets. According to legend, the ship vanished into a mysterious fog hundreds of years ago, along with its treasure.

Ella, a brave and curious third grader, decided to uncover the truth. With her trusty compass, a map she found in her grandmother's attic, and her best friend Max, they set off on an adventure that would lead them to the unexpected.

Following clues hidden in old sea shanties and landmarks, Ella and Max discovered the shipwreck of The Phantom Wave on a hidden beach. To their astonishment, the ship was not cursed but had been trapped in time, with the crew in deep sleep.

The treasure? A library of ancient books telling the world's forgotten stories. The real curse was ignorance, and the treasure was knowledge. Ella and Max decided to share this with their village, awakening the crew and breaking the curse.

Their adventure showed everyone in Seabreeze that sometimes, the greatest treasure is learning and sharing stories. The Phantom Wave set sail once again, with Ella and Max as honorary crew members, ready to discover lost tales and share them with the world.

Treasure of Tales

- Write your own short adventure story.
- What mysterious place do you discover, and what treasure do you find?

_____

_____

_____

_____

_____

_____

Voyage of Discovery

- Discuss the theme of "knowledge as treasure."
- How does this idea change Ella and Max's view of the world?

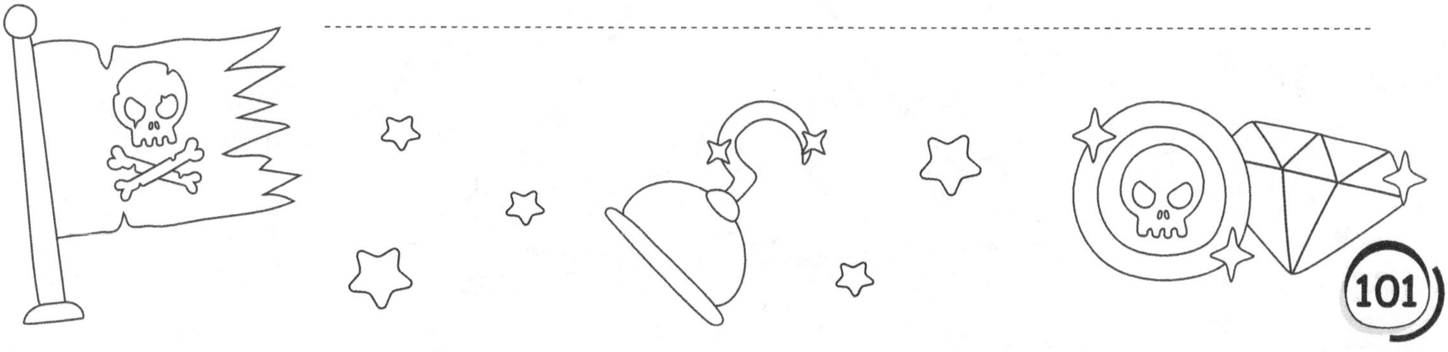

_____

_____

_____

_____

Natural Disasters: Volcanoes

Story 49

RI.3.1, RI.3.3, RI.3.7

In the small, vibrant town of Ridgeview, nestled at the foot of Mount Whisper, life was peaceful. The townspeople had heard legends of the mountain's fiery past but had never witnessed an eruption themselves. Among them was Alex, a curious third grader with a passion for science.

One sunny morning, while exploring near the mountain, Alex noticed unusual steam rising from its peak and a slight tremor underfoot. Remembering his lessons on volcanoes, he raced back to inform the town.

With the help of Alex's quick thinking, the townspeople prepared for a possible eruption. They reviewed safety plans and prepared evacuation routes, all the while Alex documented everything in his science journal.

Days passed with anxious anticipation, but thanks to their preparations, when Mount Whisper finally awoke, spewing ash and lava in a spectacular display, everyone in Ridgeview was safe. The town's swift response turned what could have been a disaster into a powerful lesson on the importance of knowledge and preparedness.

In the aftermath, Alex's journal became a key educational resource for the town. His observations and the community's response served as a testament to the power of learning and teamwork in the face of nature's challenges.

Volcano Safety Plan

- Create a safety checklis for preparing your town for a volcanic eruption.
- What steps would you take to ensure everyone's safety?

Checklist

Mount Whisper's Eruption

- Draw a scene from the story showing Mount Whisper erupting.
- Include the town's preparedness efforts in your illustration.

Story 50

The Grand Finale: The Adventure of the Lost World

RL.3.10, RL.3.3, RL.3.5, W.3.2

In the heart of the dense Rainforest Riddles, young explorers Mia and Leo stumbled upon a map leading to the Lost World, a hidden valley filled with wonders unseen by modern eyes. Their hearts raced with excitement as they envisioned discovering animals and plants no one else knew existed.

The journey was filled with challenges. They navigated through thick vines, crossed rushing rivers, and solved ancient puzzles that protected the valley. Along the way, they encountered creatures thought to be extinct, which Mia sketched and Leo wrote about in their adventure journal.

Their biggest challenge came when they reached a vast chasm. The map showed no way across, but Mia noticed a pattern of stones that matched constellations in the sky. By stepping on the stones in the right order, a hidden bridge appeared, leading them to the Lost World.

Inside the valley, they discovered a vibrant ecosystem thriving in harmony. They realized the importance of keeping this place a secret to protect it from the outside world. With heavy hearts but a sense of duty, they left the valley as they found it, taking only memories and their journal.

Back home, their story of adventure and discovery inspired their classmates to appreciate and protect the wonders of our world, even those not yet found.

Journey Through the Jungle

- Write your own adventure story about discovering a hidden place.
- What challenges do you face, and what wonders do you find?

_____

_____

_____

_____

_____

_____

_____

Mapping the Stars

- Draw the scene where Mia and Leo discover the hidden bridge.
- Include the star-patterned stones and the bridge appearing.

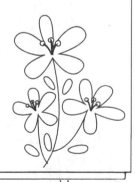

Hidden Valley Exploration

- Imagine you are exploring the hidden valley with Mia and Leo.
- Describe the most amazing plant or animal you discover.
- Why is it special? How do you think it has stayed hidden for so long?

_____
_____
_____
_____
_____
_____
_____

Bonus Audio! + Answer Key

Enhance your child's learning journey with the bonus audio for each story in this book.

Here's how your child will benefit:

- **Enhanced Understanding:** Listening to the stories improves comprehension and retention of the material.
- **Multisensory Learning:** Combining reading with listening caters to different learning styles, helping children grasp concepts more effectively.
- **Flexible Access:** Whether in the car, at home, or during a quiet classroom activity, these audio stories make it easy for children to practice reading skills without needing a book in hand—perfect for busy families and active kids.
- **Pronunciation and Fluency:** Hearing stories read aloud helps children learn proper pronunciation and develop reading fluency.
- **Engaging Content:** Captivating audio narrations bring the stories to life, making learning more interactive and fun.
- **Support for Struggling Readers:** Audio support can assist children who find reading challenging, allowing them to follow along and build confidence.

Common Core Standards

Key Ideas and Details

- **RL.3.1:** Ask and answer questions to understand a text, referring to the text.
- **RL.3.2:** Recount stories and determine the central message or moral.
- **RL.3.3:** Describe characters and explain how their actions contribute to the story.
- **RI.3.1:** Ask and answer questions to demonstrate understanding of a text, referring explicitly to the text.
- **RI.3.2:** Determine the main idea of a text; recount the key details and explain how they support the main idea.
- **RI.3.3:** Describe the relationship between a series of historical events, scientific ideas or concepts, or steps in technical procedures in a text, using language that pertains to time, sequence, and cause/effect.

Craft and Structure

- **RL.3.4:** Determine the meaning of words and phrases, distinguishing literal from nonliteral language.
- **RL.3.5:** Refer to parts of stories, dramas, and poems; describe how each part builds on earlier sections.
- **RL.3.6:** Distinguish personal point of view from that of the narrator or characters.
- **RI.3.4:** Determine the meaning of general academic and domain-specific words and phrases in a text relevant to a grade 3 topic or subject area.
- **RI.3.5:** Use text features and search tools (e.g., key words, sidebars, hyperlinks) to locate information relevant to a given topic efficiently.
- **RI.3.6:** Distinguish their own point of view from that of the author of a text.

Integration of Knowledge and Ideas

- **RL.3.7:** Explain how illustrations contribute to the story.
- **RL.3.9:** Compare and contrast themes, settings, and plots of stories by the same author.
- **RI.3.7:** Use information gained from illustrations (e.g., maps, photographs) and the words in a text to demonstrate understanding of the text (e.g., where, when, why, and how key events occur).
- **RI.3.9:** Compare and contrast the most important points and key details presented in two texts on the same topic.

Range of Reading and Level of Text Complexity

- **RL.3.10:** By the end of the year, read and comprehend literature, including stories, dramas, and poetry, at the high end of the grades 2-3 text complexity band.
- **RI.3.10:** By the end of the year, read and comprehend informational texts, including history/social studies, science, and technical texts, at the high end of the grades 2-3 text complexity band.

Foundational Skills

- **RF.3.3:** Know and apply grade-level phonics and word analysis skills in decoding words.
- **RF.3.4:** Read with sufficient accuracy and fluency to support comprehension.
- **RF.3.4.A:** Read grade-level text with purpose and understanding.
- **RF.3.4.B:** Read grade-level prose and poetry orally with accuracy, appropriate rate, and expression.
- **RF.3.4.C:** Use context to confirm or self-correct word recognition and understanding.

Could you spare just a minute?

Our biggest joy comes from helping little ones flourish and discover the world around them through learning.

That's why your thoughts matter so much to us!

Your honest thoughts about our book, even a quick sentence or two, would mean the world. We really mean it!

You'd be making a big difference for a small education brand like ours, run with love by a mother-daughter team.

Your reviews help us reach more curious minds across the globe, paving their way to success in their educational journey.

And hey, maybe we'll even sell a few more books in the process!

Every single review makes our hearts swell with gratitude.

Ready to make our day?

Scan the QR Code below to share your thoughts.

Made in United States
Cleveland, OH
18 June 2025